The Miracle Man

My Walk Through
LeUKEmia 2:18

Anthony M. Davis

The Miracle Man

My Walk Through
LeUKEmia 2:18

CONTENTS

ACKNOWLEDGMENTS

A friend once told me that going through this experience meant that God trusted me, and (in the end) He KNEW that I would give Him all the **Glory**, **Honor**, and **Praise**. Considering the magnitude of my former condition, it is impossible to think I survived it alone. **God** provided an enormous amount of assistance and guidance. The term that describes His work is no less than a "miracle."

Since day one, God has been with me, and I thank Him eternally for trusting me and surrounding me with an abundance of saints. There are many to mention, and I want to acknowledge everyone involved for their unfailing obedience to God's will in my life. My multitude of "thanks" goes as follows:

To my wife, **Felicia**, your *"spiritual panic"* saved my life! Your heart is incredible, and it has been phenomenal for me to have a front-row seat watching God's good works in you. You may think one way about yourself in certain areas, but I think the complete opposite – you are a ROCK – a solid foundation for our family, and I thank God daily for your existence.

To my daughter, **Hannah**, for being there when your mother asked. While she was with me in the hospital, you stepped up and helped with your brothers. I have watched you become the epitome of your birthstone - a diamond, and there is tremendous greatness in you. Trust the gifts God has implanted in you and continue to be a brilliant gem.

To my oldest son, **Jaiden**, thank you for the vision. You are an extraordinary young man with a heart to match, and I have not even gotten to your special gift (that is another book). Nobody knows this, but when you were born, my nickname for you was "The Truth," and son, you are.

Landon, my youngest, thank you for being you. When Minister Gilda Harris first laid eyes on you, she declared,

"New Life," and you are. Continue to interrupt me and allow God to show me how to pause and appreciate the gift of life.

Hannah, Jaiden, and Landon, your gifts are different, but I love you all equally for how you operate in them.

To **Glenn**, my brother, your selfless "donation" defies any gratitude I can express in words. You stepped up big for your baby brother. And **Valorie** – thank you for lending part of your husband to me. I appreciate you both for the time spent at the clinic relieving Felicia, the visits to the hospital, and at the apartment in Durham. I guess there was a good reason you guys moved to Durham.

To my **mother**, my sister, **Kathy**, and my niece **Daniella**: thank you for traveling down from New York to North Carolina to spend quality time, talk, and laugh. It gave us beautiful moments to focus on life and family as God concentrated on my healing.

Aunt Emma, thank you for your love, support, and caring for Landon when we were in the apartment, and he could not stay with us. You and Kiya were an enormous help.

Helen and **Andre**, my sister and brother-in-law, thank you for your prayers. Helen, your calming voice was genuinely comforting. When Felicia and I agreed to get treated at Wake Forest Baptist, you confirmed it by first allowing God to speak through you, and then you told us, "Go see what they have to say."

To my sister, **Ann**: I know it was rough hearing that your baby brother had cancer, but when Felicia asked me who in the family to call first, I told her you. I have relied on your wisdom a lot over the years, and I thank you for being that non-judgmental ear when I needed someone to hear about decisions I have made, good or bad.

To **Vanessa Griffith, Mother Jarvis, Clothel Jarvis, Marjorie Faustin, Kera Wilson, Ron** and **Paula Divers** and (once again) **Hannah**, thank you for taking care of my boys. It is difficult for children when a parent is unavailable. It was beautiful to have you all step in for us or to (at least) distract them.

Pastor and First Lady, Rev. Dr. Michael L. Henderson, and Rev. Dr. Twanna Henderson: your guidance has been incredible. Your combined leadership prepared me for my miracle walk. Thank you for your prayers and for being my "spiritual parents." May God continue to strengthen you and allow you to develop more Kingdom Warriors.

Rev. Paulus Ford, and **Min. Tonja Ford** - my brother and sister in Christ, you are family. You two have embraced us ever since we were a part of your Life Group. Rev. Paulus, you have been a great mentor - allowing me to grow in my purpose. The words you told me (and I am paraphrasing), "Take care of what you have, and God will trust you with more," still resonate with me today. Thank you both for standing in for Felicia and hanging out with me in the hospital (300!!!).

Donnie Saunders: thank you for holding me accountable for my "written" testimony of this miracle, my friend. Always asking me, "How's the book going?" and years later, here it is! Thank you for standing in for Felicia and hanging out with me in the hospital (M&M Peanuts)!!

Thank you to my friend, **Herb Downing**, for stepping in and holding it down for Felicia; it was great fellowshipping with you. I look forward to our continued NY Yankees talks and hanging out with you and Geraldine. Love you guys.

Life Group: thank you for all the love, prayers, and support. Your obedience to what God called you to do for my family and me is heartfelt. Continue to press, and God will Bless!!!

A shout out of appreciation to my **ministries: Altar Counsel**, **KLI** (Youth), **Marriage**, and **Men's**, for the love, prayers, and visits. You are proof that ministry extends outside the walls of the building.

To the congregation of **New Beginnings Church** in Matthews, NC: I am grateful for your service – it is like no other. When our calls went out, your prayers penetrated my heart. We felt your love throughout our journey. Felicia's co-worker guided us to you, and in February 2009, we became members. Ministry exploded within us, and God expanded our territory. Thank you for being obedient in your calling and participating in our spiritual assignment. May God continue to Bless you.

To my manager at work, **James Paulin**: since my diagnosis in August 2016 - until my return to work a year later, you kept in contact with Felicia and preserved my job. For that, I am forever grateful.

To my (present and former) co-workers: **Vinnie Rivera**, **Troy Tatum**, **Ken Lewis**, and **Jason Willard**, taking time to travel to the hospital for visits showed me how meaningful our relationship in the office has been to you.

Vinnie, I praise God for you and how you embraced me from the start at TIAA, for you and Sharon hanging out with Felicia and me, for allowing me to renew your and Sharon's vows, and for chillin' with me at Duke (shoot, I almost forgot the conferences). God Bless you and your family.

Troy, thank you and Angela for an on-time word at the hospital and our unofficial bible studies in the office. Maintain your walk in God's Word, and He will continue blessing people through your voice. May God always bless you and your family.

Ken, you go above and beyond as a friend, and I thank you for stopping by Wake Forest and forgetting your hat. Forever lead with your heart and stop swinging 9020s.

Jason, your visit alone almost surprised the leukemia out of me! Thank you for reminding me of our friendship and the fun times at work. God Bless you.

And to the host of additional co-workers at **TIAA** who took the time to ask about me, send a card, or stay on the phone with me for two hours (**Gio**), I value you all.

Finally, thanks to **Hopematch.org** for supporting my family during my healing time. I appreciate your blessings. God has and will continue to bestow good things upon your organization.

The Lord has performed numerous acts of greatness during my assignment. So great that I began to call leukemia my "blessing." I offer ceaseless thanks to Him for considering me, being with me, and guiding me through this journey.

INTRODUCTION

And all who heard it were amazed about the things which were told them by the shepherds.

Luke 2:18

Dictionary.com defines a miracle as *"an effect or extraordinary event in the physical world that surpasses all known human or natural powers and is ascribed to a supernatural cause."* What looks impossible becomes possible.

After my initial battle with leukemia, I attended a Tuesday night Bible Study. It was the first since my diagnosis. Pastor walked down the aisle per usual, but he did not notice Felicia and me on the end seats. At the close of praise and worship, he approached the podium and was about to pray, but before doing so, he looked at me and asked, "Minister Anthony, is that you?" When I motioned affirmatively, he told the congregation what I went through, and at that moment, he entitled me the *"Miracle*

Man." It took a while to embrace it; I am not a fan of being in the spotlight, but a friend in ministry reminded me that what I experienced was indeed a miracle.

Leukemia is a tough fight. Like most cancers, it has a high rate of defeating its victims. I needed to realize that God was speaking *through* Pastor when he used the word "miracle" pertaining to myself; it made it easier to receive the moniker after witnessing several people who had succumbed to this disease.

The book's subtitle was something that came to me when I was in the hospital. Phonetically speaking, Leukemia has the book of Luke in its first half – I felt it was an appropriate way to honor God. But what scripture would I use? Then God spoke to me, "Your birthday." I looked up Luke 2:18, which states: "And all who heard it were amazed....".

While I was in the hospital, both at Wake Forrest Baptist and Duke University, the doctors and the nurses would stand in amazement at my progress, proclaiming that they had never seen anything like this. My doctor at Duke, Dr. Lopez, even brought one of his colleagues in to view me. I describe their expressions as being awestruck!

Like the shepherds in the above verse, Dr. Lopez told all because he was amazed and needed a witness so that others would believe. I hope my testimony provides anyone who reads it with more profound insight that God is in the business of miracles. He is a God of yesterday, today, and always.

CHAPTER 0
BACKGROUND

In the beginning was the Word, and the Word was with God, and the Word was God.

John 1:1

The hardest thing for me to do when I write is the opening because when I write papers, I tend to skip the beginning and go directly to the "meat" of what I am trying to express. Even when I began writing this book, old habits took me to the meat, BUT God. God told me I needed to start before the Leukemia, and it suddenly made sense. He made me slow down and ask myself, "How can anyone reading this understand some of my decisions, the way I process things, or even the "Why" behind my "Why?" it would probably be harder for them to comprehend without background.

Throughout this book, God wants me to express how I walked this thing out and show others what He did for me by using my life experiences in connection to the Word. When situations arise, I use scriptures that seem relative to my case. I observed how characters in the Bible were similarly tested and then meditated on what they would do to bring resolve. I pray that you will connect with my story and become encouraged to *Biblically* identify your challenges and see what the Word says to you on how to confront your life's concerns.

Now I never compare myself to Jesus, but John 1:1 helps the believer prove to the non-believer that Jesus (the Word) existed in the beginning. It gives background knowledge of the Trinity - that God the Father, Son, and the Holy Spirit always existed. This chapter intends not to prove that I existed but rather to give some personal history of me before Leukemia. I will spotlight specific experiences over my 49 years that impacted me so profoundly that they helped me fight the battle of my life. It brings light to an understanding of my faith, love, hope, and empathy towards others, but mostly my JOY that I will not allow Satan to steal.

The following may be hard to believe, but it is true. When I was a very young child - still sleeping in a crib - I vividly remember the moment my spirit permeated my flesh. I also recall life episodes that flashed before my eyes – comparable to the opening credits of a Marvel film (Ok, let me give you some time to stop laughing, but this was the best way I could provide reference).

One event involved a snake in our home, and my oldest sister, Helen, quickly snatched me up to move me away from it. When I was older, I asked her about that day, and Helen confirmed that it happened - exactly as I described! Remembering these occurrences so clearly - at such an early age - cemented my belief that someone greater was always here with me. Some adults are still searching, but I already knew my life had a particular reason back then. And God placed me in the arms of Ralph and Constance Davis to discover and ultimately thrive in that purpose.

As I reflect on my youth, my parents were great; not perfect, but great. And like many others, they had no formal classes in parenthood, just two good folks doing what they knew best. They learned in succession – meaning, each child from eldest to youngest (Helen, Bubba (Ralph, JR.) Glenn, Kathy, and Ann) were preparing them for the next until they got to child six, ME! By then, the Davis' had finally perfected how to raise a child, or they were just plain tired.

When I tell people about my upbringing, they are dumbfounded when I inform them that I was never spanked, yelled at, or put on punishment…EVER! If you ask my brothers and sisters about their experiences growing up in the same household - under the SAME tutelage, you will probably get five different lifelong encounters. As for this kid, I enjoyed my parents, siblings, and the time spent living in our various abodes. Being the youngest also gave me a different perspective; I had little to no responsibilities, and all I could see was that seven loving people were looking after Anthony!

I am told we lived in a house during my first year of life, although I have no recollection of this, and I never get the same story from my family. I have a private joke with my mother – I always tell her that I was the _only_ person (out of all eight of us) who never lived in a house growing up. She takes the humor in stride because she knows how incredibly grateful I am for where and how I grew up. The importance was not whether I was raised in a house versus the projects; the essence was that I grew up with my entire family. We were not flawless; we were LOVED.

For instance, "The Fall" is an infamous story from the Davis house about which my sister, Kathy, and my brother, Glenn, have debates. I was a novice at walking then, and I believe my parents were out. Until now, neither Kathy nor Glenn will admit who was responsible for watching me in my parent's absence. I know that three of us were upstairs at one moment, and there were only two at the next. Unfortunately for me, I was not one of them. The only conclusion my elder siblings agreed upon was how quickly they figured out I had a hard head! I wish I had more Davis "HOUSE" chronicles to share, but I guess that knock on my skull was enough trauma for one year. Moving right along…

Often, God directs us to move. To our detriment, if it does not precisely align with *our* feelings, we refuse to obey and remain still. Would you intentionally leave a house for the projects - going from owner to tenant? My parents made a change that would impact themselves and their children. My father and mother lost the house, and we had to move into the Baisley Park Projects in South Jamaica, Queens, New York. For them, readjusting and downsizing to the confines of "the projects" must have been challenging physically and emotionally, but they did what they had to do. I am not sure how my siblings felt about the move, but it was the most impactful decision my parents made for me.

We lived in Building #1 of five, on the first floor, in apartment 1D. We were eight-deep in a four-bedroom, one-bath dwelling! These living conditions formed my early perception of the family construct. Have you ever realized how (sometimes) parents will inadvertently stumble into genius and, while falling, have no immediate sense of the greater good they have accomplished? Our bedroom organization is proof of that subconsciousness.

My mother and father slept in the room closest to the door. Kathy and Ann were in the next over. Bubba

(Ralph Jr.), Glenn, and I were in the most significantly sized one, and Helen, the firstborn, occupied the last. As you can imagine, we were very closely situated and had to be very creative - especially regarding bathroom time.

Back then, the children thought the arrangement was to ensure none of us could sneak out (which *would* have been a genius move from my parents); however, that was not the intent. The original plan was to accommodate an eight-member family comfortably and logistically, but as a bonus, the children still could not sneak out. Therefore, how our parents organized limited space for our general comfort turned into an unintended stroke of genius!

As previously stated, I jokingly complained about not living in a house; I am grateful that my formative years were in the projects. And coming from a family who once lived in a house, I will never broadly declare that the nature of homeowners is better than that of renters - I have seen both. The type of building you reside in does not define you but WHO lives in you does.

So, I ask, WHO is the TENANT in your dwelling?

It is logical to think that most people would know and get along (with one another) in a close and similar environment. However, living in Baisley was strange. Instead of being located on one side of the street, the five structures were separated on either side of New York Boulevard (later renamed Guy R. Brewer Boulevard). This street not only split buildings, but it also split people.

Ours and the adjacent building were the only ones I bothered to familiarize myself with. I never ventured across the street to the others out of fear - a fear which stemmed solely from lack of knowledge. To me, it was foreign territory. My trepidation placed me in a figurative box, and it (likely) prevented me from experiencing the friendship of other great families.

A good set of the "box" mentality (living prominent and *rent-free* in the minds of project dwellers or anyone else) is self-inflicted. You go to school, work, get groceries, (maybe) go to church, and then come home. The next day or week, this cycle is repeated. You become complacent with what you do and have, eventually lacking desires that are further than your heart can feel or your eyes can see. If the neighborhood hustler has a nice car, clothes, and money, and you allow the method by which these goals were attained to be your goals, too, you allow someone else to be your "vision" when there is so much more to behold, and lawful ways to obtain them.

Thankfully, my parents made sure we embarked beyond the box. We would go to game shows when they were filmed in New York. My sister Ann, my cousin Tommy and I were part of a studio audience for a children's program called "Wonderamma." We grew up seeing the city and its beautiful sites - including the

Empire State Building and the Twin Towers. We would attend Broadway Shows like "The Wiz" and "Dreamgirls." We went to Rockaway Playland and Rye Playland. And we experienced all of this without a car! So, never let anyone put limits on you. You are your only limit; what stops you is the will to fight.

How much are you willing to fight for yourself and God's vision that He implanted in you?

I find it curious how I managed to embody all God's gifts in my life. I am blessed to have grown up with seven personalities to observe - pulling out the good pieces (never complained about the bad) and framing them all into one unique character. My family nurtured me as I matured - while still allowing me to be me. There was a particular dichotomy between treating me like "the baby" but, on the other hand, not.

My relationship with my dad was entirely different from that of my siblings. I do not think they were aware, but I spent most of my time with him. We did not have televisions in our bedrooms, so if we wanted to watch TV at all. We had to watch TV in the living room with Pop. Whatever he watched, we watched: the Yankees, Knicks, Mannix, Mission Impossible, Sanford & Son, and All in the Family. It made for great TV but much greater quality time.

As we grew older, the audience in the living room slimmed down until it was only Pop in his chair and me lying on the couch across from him. Looking back, I never knew how much that time meant to me, how much influence it had on me, and how much it would mold me into the man I am today. Although he was not a man of many words, his presence alone spoke volumes. Pop had excellent discernment for folks – recognizing garbage when it was in his face and directly addressing it when necessary. That leads me to what I admired most about my father: his honesty and character. And I never realized how formidable his character was until I reflected on a story with my mother.

My mother and I usually talk on the phone each Sunday after church. On one of those Sundays, we recalled an accident I was involved in.

During summertime in the mid-80s, my friends Kenny, Keith, and I used to ride our bikes all over Queens, NY. Kenny lived in Rochdale, a predominately black-owned co-op in Jamaica, Queens, NY. Coming from the projects, I found myself impressed with people who lived in co-ops because even though they were in buildings like mine, it *felt* like they were somehow set apart; it seemed different. Even when the big blackout in 1977 put everyone else at a standstill, Rochdale was unaffected; they had a generator to keep the power going.

Oh, I need to return to the story.

We hung out near Kenny's building, prepared to head home, and decided to make it a race. I cannot remember who was leading, but I *know* I was in second. The quickest way to our destination was through a path extending from Kenny's building to behind Gouz (rhymes with cows) - the community grocery market.

The path was clear, and we were speeding as we approached a hill just shy of reaching the rear of the store. Suddenly, a car pulling out in reverse hit me. I rolled off the vehicle's trunk, landed on one knee, looked down, grabbed my hat, and put it back on my head. Simultaneously, Kenny screamed my name while Keith gathered my bent-up bike. The gentleman who hit me came out of his vehicle and started to blame me for the accident until two older women walking from the other direction fiercely defended me. He quickly changed his tune. Once things simmered down, I got his contact information before walking my twisted bike home to inform my parents of the incident.

My mother immediately attempted to contact the driver with the data he provided, but he gave me the WRONG NUMBER! My sister Kathy told her boyfriend, Daryl, and he drove us to the police station to file a police report. Once there, the officer at the desk asked me to describe the car that hit me. I told them it was a black BMW with a yellow plate - of which I could only remember the first three letters. The officer informed us that no New York plate existed with that description. But I was persistent, so the officer continued to look and found a Pennsylvania plate that fit the description. To our surprise, the car belonged to the owner of Gouz. We then obtained Mr. Gouz's *CORRECT* information and found the number was only off one digit. Seeing that minor infraction, my parents decided to extend Mr. Gouz grace before meeting with him.

Kenny and I were outside when Mr. Gouz came over to negotiate a replacement price. We all were inside the apartment at one point, and my parents talked with Mr. Gouz a little before opening a Sears catalog and turning the pages to the bike section. At that moment, Kenny and I concocted an idea to pick out the most expensive one in the book. After all, Mr. Gouz needed to be taught a lesson. The scheme was to choose a bike that cost more than the one damaged. Our perspective was that he was not candid with his information, so why should we?

Also, he was the store *owner*, so the amount we were about to ask for could not possibly put a dent in his wallet. But before we could utter a word, my father took over, and we never had the chance to practice our deception. Pop negotiated a fair price, and Mr. Gouz wrote the check and exited. Disappointed in the outcome, Kenny left shortly after.

In turn, my mother retreated to my parent's bedroom, and I was hot on her heels. I was agitated. I wanted more money, and my mother happened to agree with me. Following that ordeal (the car, the accusation, the wrong info), I felt more compensation was due to me. After all, the man hit me…a child…with HIS car and expected me to apologize to him!

Pop entered the room with fists on his hips during my mini meltdown, posing like a "Ghetto Superman," and said, "I think I could have gotten more." And no sooner than he walked in to speak those words, he turned around and walked back out – but not before my mother murmured, *"You idiot."*

Mom and I finished our recollection of that summer day – chuckling at times throughout, and by the story's end, I realized how honest my father was. Even when faced with the temptation to defraud a seemingly well-to-do individual, a dishonest and insensitive man to his "baby boy," he chose righteousness. Pop's actions that day still resonate with me now. He taught me to do the right thing even when I think no one else is watching. God is omnipresent. Thank you, Pop, for being a man of integrity.

How should we treat people? I was taught the "Golden Rule" tenets- to treat people how I want to be treated. That is such a simple statement to make but sometimes tricky to obey. Walking it out is a humble, self-sacrificing, and often discreet and thankless act requiring courage. The difficulty emerges because our flesh will (sometimes) desire the opposite…admiration, selfishness, and praise. Many may wonder, "Where is the reward in that?"

Earlier, I described my father as a man of integrity. In turn, the word empathetic fits my mother from head to toe. She can understand and share the feelings of others, and she has always had kind words to say. Aside from the "idiot" comment, I have rarely heard her say *anything* negative. And above that, she would not allow cruel or demeaning words from our mouths either. Mom was continually ready to say the right things without being harsh. I imagine being the youngest paid off; my mom never raised her hand or voice to me. Heck, the only "switch" I knew about was the light switch! What I considered the worst thing she ever said to me occurred in December 1986, and it was not horrible at all.

After a challenging first year at St. John's University, I took a semester off. As time drew nearer for me to return to school, I caught the flu – possibly prolonging my absence. During that lapse, my mother was patient and supportive of me; she never asked me why I felt I needed the time away, but her mother's intuition led her to believe something below the surface was wrong that I was unwilling to discuss.

While lying in my bed feeling awful, she came into my room, looked at me, and in a clear and respectful tone said, "Next semester, either you are going back to school or getting a job." As sick as I was, all I could reply was, "OK."

Mom was keeping it real. How else could I respond, considering everything this woman had done for me? Despite my mental *and* physical condition, she understood something needed to happen… soon. I was in a "funk," and she refused to let me wallow in it. I required motivation – a driving force to work it out.

Hands down, mom was one of the most excellent managers I have ever known. She had to oversee seven distinct personalities with limited resources and space – all while residing in the projects of Queens, New York. Not dismissing the impact of my father's presence, but growing up, my mother was the heart and soul of our family. Through every year and season, she knew (individually) what we all needed, how to talk to us, and how to love on us.

We were baptized and raised Catholic. Every Sunday at 11:00 AM, if you were a child living under our roof, you attended church for one hour at St. Bonaventure in Queens, NY. Pop did not participate, and up to this day, no one has ever questioned his decision to abstain. It was never an issue. We, as children, did what we were told (for the most part) and let Pop be Pop.

In addition to the church, we also went to a Catholic school, St. Catherine of Sienna in St. Albans, Queens. That is where my "blind faith" and understanding of the *"why"* we believe in Christ took root.

I have revealed some knowledge about who I am as a person. God had to put me with a family that could help me develop into the man He considered necessary to serve an intended audience. I was taught gratefulness, unity, integrity, empathy, patience, faith, understanding,

41

self-actualization, motivation, and perseverance. Each quality prepared me for defeating Leukemia and writing this book to inspire others.

God plants each of us where He needs us. We can complain about our situations but remember that He will not keep us there. And however odd as it sounds, we ALL have an audience that God requires us to reach after a storm. Deal with your *Chapter Zero* so you can get to Chapter One.

CHAPTER 1
Have You Considered?

The Lord said to Satan, "Have you considered My servant Job? For there is no one like him on the earth, a blameless and upright man, fearing God and turning away from evil."
Job 1:8

Job was the best of the best - a righteous man. Righteous people are not always right; they just try to do the right thing. God bore in mind this honest man because He knew He could trust him. That is what happens when you are *considered*. Phrases like, "Look at him," "Isn't she the cutest?" "That boy is good!" God is talking about you, and the same as any noble parent, He is proud of you. When God considers you, make Him proud.

When they entered, he looked at Eliab and thought, "Surely the Lord's anointed is before Him." But the Lord said to Samuel, "Do not look at his appearance or at the height of his stature, because I have rejected him; for God sees not as man sees, for man looks at the outward appearance, but the Lord looks at the heart." Then Jesse called Abinadab and made him pass before Samuel. And he said, "The Lord has not chosen this one either." Next, Jesse made Shammah pass by. And he said, "The Lord has not chosen this one either." Thus, Jesse made seven of his sons pass before Samuel. But Samuel said to Jesse, "The Lord has not chosen these." And Samuel said to Jesse, "Are these all the children?" And he said, "There remains yet the youngest, and behold, he is tending the sheep." Then Samuel said to Jesse, "Send and bring him, for we will not sit down until he comes here." So, he sent and brought him in. Now he was ruddy, with beautiful eyes and a handsome appearance. And the Lord said, "Arise, anoint him; for this is he."

1 Samuel 16:6-12

This anointed young boy would become a king, and his name was David – imperfect, yet still considered for greatness…he was a man "after God's own heart." (1 Samuel: 13-14)

June 2016: I firmly believe anything in the Bible can happen again today. Job was a man of God who reverenced Him and did the right thing. One of my pet peeves is that people on this Earth do not at least *try* to do the right thing. Even worse, as BELIEVERS, we feel that just accepting Jesus as Lord and Savior is enough. Why are we only *sometimes* trying to do the right thing? I can only imagine how Job and David felt before they were considered.

Okay, I stepped down from my soapbox, but I believe that in June 2016, God saw the devil roaming about the earth in my neighborhood and asked him if he considered His servant Anthony. Not that I do everything right all the time or even sometimes, but I at least try to. I wish I could prove it to you, but I cannot. I can declare that God knows my heart - whether He views me in or outside my home. My marriage, family, job, and church were good, and my relationship with my Lord and Savior was VERY GOOD! But all that was about to change three weeks later.

On **July 23, 2016**, I traveled home with my wife and our boys from a family reunion in Columbia, SC. It was a straight, 90min highway drive up I-77 North, and I felt awful. I was tired, had a slight headache, and was a little "out" of it. I am familiar with the symptoms of dehydration - that is what it felt like, so I initially brushed it off. Once we arrived home, I drank fluids and rested. Eventually, those signs went away, and another group came. I thought the subsequent symptoms were allergies, but I sought professional treatment, and the Urgent Care provider diagnosed them as a sinus infection. I was prescribed medication and instructed to take a couple of days off.

I followed the advice and took those days from work but going to work became a massive struggle for me over the next couple of weeks. I felt horrible on my drives to and from. I would get to my desk, rest for a while, feel ok, get home, and go to bed exhausted -most of the time with a headache. This new routine put a strain on my family because they expected our typical and constant hubby/daddy interactions with each other right after work and me being the last one to go to bed. Instead, I was depleted, stand-offish, and the first to bed.

*But let me digress for a minute –

On Friday, **January 17, 2014**, I had just returned from a business conference held by my employer in Orlando, Florida, where we stayed at a beautiful hotel called the Swan and Dolphin. I was excited to share the details of this incredible trip with my best friend, Matt Shingler, my youngest son's godfather.

After the sessions were completed on Thursday, everyone boarded charter buses, and they drove us to the back entrance of Disney's Epcot Center. We were escorted through the park to what looked like a hangar, where we were greeted by waiters and waitresses flanked on both sides. They were all holding trays of beer and wine. Now at a different time in my life, I would have been in heaven seeing all the libations, but I gave up drinking when I decided to be in ministry. No one *told* me to stop drinking, and I do not see anything wrong with a drink here or there, but I would never want anyone to move away from God because of optics that could appear contrary to my calling.

When I entered the hangar, I felt like a VIP. All the food I could eat, an open bar, a DJ, and a dance floor set up like the one from the iconic movie "Saturday Night Fever" (Google it). I was straight "tripping!" At 9 PM, everything inside stopped, and we were taken outdoors to a roped-off area near the pond to watch the fireworks display. It was a fantastic night, and I could not *wait* to tell my friend about it.

Matt and I were like an interchangeable Batman and Robin duo, each able to either take the lead or follow the other when called to. Matt was white, and I only bring up his color because he looked at me one day and said, "Ant, you're the whitest black guy I've ever known." In turn, I said, "Matt, you're the blackest white guy I have ever known." Our bond was so unique that we could say *anything* to each other. At times we would disagree, but still, we could come back and enjoy each other's presence. We had fun sharing and celebrating our experiences as well as our families. All the more reason I was so excited to get back and tell him about my Orlando trip. But sadly, I never got a chance.

Once home, Felicia informed me that Matt had week-long migraine headaches. His wife, Tangie, was concerned about the duration, so Felicia suggested that she not wait any longer and take him to the emergency room. Matt was prone to having migraines, so we all thought it was nothing too severe and assumed everything was ok.

On the same day Tangie took Matt to be evaluated, Felicia had gone to an all-night prayer vigil at church, and I was home working on a project. During the vigil, Tangie contacted Felicia and told her the results…it was a brain tumor. Matt was immediately admitted to the hospital. Felicia told First Lady Twanna Henderson, and they started interceding on his behalf.

When Felicia told me, I stopped what I was doing and cried for what seemed to be a full hour. All I could think about was Tangie and the kids. I could not sleep. I cried all night. It was like the minute I heard cancer; I heard *death*. Not that I lacked faith or hope, but all I could imagine in my head at that moment was losing my best friend. The next day, we visited him.

I have a low tolerance for hospitals; they can be very depressing. And my friend was lying in one preparing for the battle of his life. I was supposed to be in his presence to uplift and encourage him, but I was so emotionally empty; how could I do that? How could I encourage my friend while being discouraged? But it was not about me; this was for Matt. Who cares if I am depressed? I have the gift of exhortation, so I had to suck it up and deliver for Matt. The walk to Matt's room felt like the most extended trek I have ever experienced, and the seemingly ample time during that walk still did not help me figure out what to say or do. As I turned into his room, I took a deep breath, walked in, and saw his big smile.

He was acting like…like regular old' Matt! I thought it would be a sad visit, but we laughed boisterously while this man was literally on his sick bed. In contrast, most people would be down in the dumps, but not Matt; this man chuckled at death. "Victory" was all over his face. He was the one who was sick, and we were supposed to be encouraging him, yet he was uplifting us – showing no fear of his upcoming task. The following week Matt had an operation to remove the tumor. Despite the journey he was confronting and unaware of the outcome, he managed to exude absolute JOY! Matt knew WHO was in control. Even though this *looked* fatal, he understood that there was a purpose for this tumor. By August 2015, he was admitted back into the hospital.

Another close friend of ours, Kevin Rivers, called me, and we talked about Matt and his condition. It was now October 2015, and I had a candid conversation with Kevin. I told him what I was fervently praying to God for regarding Matt. I told him that I said to God, "Whatever Your Will is, do it quickly. Either heal him or call him home" (I did not lose hope, I just wanted my friend to be at peace). A few minutes after I told Kevin about my prayer, Tangie called Kevin and told him Matt had passed.

We always ask, "Why does God let good people die young?" Matt was only 36! He was a great man of God, a dedicated husband and father, and a loyal friend. Why? It might be that He will still go after that "one" who does not know Him. One of Tangie's cousins gave his life to Christ at Matt's homegoing ceremony. That following weekend, he was shot to death. Would Tangie's cousin have given his life to Christ if Matt was still alive? We will never know. But we understand, as believers, that to be absent from the body is to be present with the Lord. That was one "why"; another "why" would come soon.

I have been a member of New Beginnings Church since February 2009. At New Beginnings, before you are given the title of Minister, you must go through Ministers in Training (M.I.T.). I spent over two years training under Rev. Dr. Michael L. Henderson (our pastor), and during that time, I bonded with some of the members in class. Of course, Matt (far left) was one, and another was Trent Knight (far right).

Trent and I are tight. "We ride together; we cried together… Bad Boys for Life!". Ooops, wrong story. Nonetheless, he is another cool guy. He is very soft-spoken and has a gentle tone to his voice, but do not mistake his mildness for weakness. Trent knows how to say "no," and it would not be wise to try to deceive him. He keeps it 100% *all* the time.

After graduation, Trent progressed in church and was considered for an eldership. His title went from Minister to Elder-Elect. As with Matt, Trent and I could talk for hours about work, family, or church life, but we would mainly talk about media and video concerns. He was over the Media Ministry at the time, and when needed, I created video content for the Sunday announcements.

Pictured left to right: Matt, Jeffrey Baker, myself, Valerie Watkins, Susie Stevens, Jason Thomas, Camica McKnight, Rose Hamilton, Tim Livingston, Clothel Jarvis, Belinda Thomas, and Trent.

One day in May of 2016, Trent texted me and wanted to meet me in his office before Bible Study. I was nervous because we usually talk on the phone or in passing, so setting up a meeting before Bible Study perplexed me. I was like, "Huh? My mind went directly to extreme opposite rationales. I immediately thought, "I must have done something wrong ministerially," or "they are about to hire me full-on." Either way, I had my answer prepared… it was a resounding "No." Regardless of my theories at that moment, I knew Trent had *something* important to tell me, and I just had to exercise patience to find out.

Our Bible Study is every Tuesday at 12 noon and 7 PM. I planned to meet Trent around 6:30 PM so we could talk before the evening session. I went to his office in the Ministry Center and knocked on his door; he called me inside; I entered and sat down. I am convinced he said more than what I am about to tell you, but honestly, all I heard registering to my ears from his mouth was, "I have cancer." I lost it! Why God? Why are You allowing Satan to consider yet *another* one of my friends? Matt passed away seven months earlier; how could You let Trent become diagnosed with cancer too? You expect me to serve Your people, but instead, it felt like You were determined to hand me another burden!

My mind was a mangled wreck! That is until Trent, with his reassuring voice, said, "Don't worry, everything will be alright." He calmly explained the treatment he would receive, and I eventually arrived at the impression that everything *would* be alright, but at the same time, I *still* wondered why God would allow me to get so close to these two men.

Many questions were floating around in my head. Matt and Trent were great men and outstanding friends. Why did they have to go through this? They were both secure in their belief in Jesus as their Lord and Savior. My "circle" had been infiltrated; I *had* to take this personally. God, what are You trying to tell me? What am I supposed to receive from this sorrow and pain?

Weeks after our talk, Trent had a successful operation to remove the cancerous cells from his prostate; he has been in remission ever since. I then asked myself jokingly, "Who's next?" As strange as it was for two close friends to develop cancer, God was preparing me for something through it. And with God, *nothing* is coincidental. Matt, Trent, and I were not the "spotlight-seeking" type; we served not to be recognized but for God to be glorified and to edify our "audiences." What was God trying to show me in watching my close friends battle these cancers, and most importantly, why?

CHAPTER 2
The Prophecy

In those days, Hezekiah became mortally ill. And Isaiah the prophet, the son of Amoz, came to him and said to him, "Thus says the Lord, 'Set your house in order, for you shall die and not live.'"

Isaiah 38:1

As mentioned earlier, we attend New Beginnings Church in Matthews, NC, and we have a sizeable congregation. Large churches can become out of touch with their congregants during growth. Not wanting that to be a probability for us, Pastor Henderson decided to implement something called "Life Groups or Small Groups" into our regimen as a way for us to make the interactions in our church feel more personal - regardless of size. Pastor has often referred to them as the church's "Best-kept secret" because participation in these groups helps extend the church and develops lifelong friendships that become extended family.

These groups gather every other Thursday evening (from February to June) at several members' homes around the city. We would eat, sing, fellowship, and read through a Christ-centered book that we would discuss. We also would choose an outreach project to spread the love of Christ from the inside of the church walls and outside into the surrounding communities.

Our first Life Group was at Reverend Paulus and Minister Tonja Ford's home. *Amazing* people! There, I was genuinely developed as a minister, and I am grateful to have learned essential and enduring lessons under their tutelage. At the end of every Life Group season, the groups would come together at our Tuesday night Bible Studies and present their outreach projects in front of the congregation.

Most groups would describe their projects via short speeches, but not Ford's Life Group. Rev. Paulus knew I had hidden talents, and God told him to expose my gifts – the ability to produce something different yet still as powerful and engaging as the others; Rev. Paulus asked me to create a *visual* presentation; he would go up alone, ask our group to stand together to be recognized/introduced to everyone, and then instruct the audience members to pay attention to the screens where our presentation would show. I guess I was pretty good at that type of media because, throughout the years, other groups have asked me to create their presentations for them as well. By February 2014, with the help of Rev. Paulus's mentoring, I eventually branched off and facilitated the Davis Life Group.

Certain things in life you remember like it was yesterday - regardless of when they occurred. On **August 16, 2016**, we viewed outreach presentations for that season. Usually, our sons would attend children's church –not far from the room where we were, but on this particular night, my oldest son Jaiden stayed with us in the Ministry Center Sanctuary. While watching the speeches, Felicia told me that Jaiden was crying. I looked at him, and he was inconsolable. I leaned in to ask him what was wrong, but he would not respond. I told him to *try* to stop crying, and we would talk about it in the car on the way home. He eventually stopped crying, and we continued to watch the presentations.

After Bible Study, we got in the car, and I asked Jaiden why he was crying earlier. Jaiden said, "I had a vision." Most children do not use the word vision; they say dream. Jaiden said VISION. When I heard those words, I knew I had to listen. In my mind, I said, "Oh, oh," because inherently, I knew the following words out of his mouth would be a message from God. I braced myself as Jaiden continued, "You went to the hospital and died."

So, ***that*** is what was wrong with me; I was dying! These past few weeks of symptoms I was experiencing were signs of me dying! Fearful of what he said, and at the same time believing my "little prophet," I had to settle down and rationally explain to him about dreams and visions.

My mother and I had a conversation about Jaiden only two weeks before. He is a special boy with a good heart. His temperament is similar to mine but better. He treats people with respect and looks out for his family. He is a child with friends from all walks of life. If (out of curiosity) we ask him what race his friends are, he asks, "Why does that matter?"

Jaiden also has this remarkable gift of drawing. Since he was four years old, he has shown outstanding abilities as an artist – creating things most adults could not master. I have seen God work through his heart and talents while he was very young, so why would He not *speak* through him too? I believe God had prepared me for Jaiden's vision because He has also spoken to *me* through visions and dreams – which allowed me to talk to Jaiden about his vision without either one of us feeling uncomfortable.

I explained to Jaiden that his vision was a clear and vital message from God to me. That God was preparing us for something that was about to happen. I explained how the vision is true but that it may not happen that quickly. Visualizing his dad being dead *had* to be traumatic, but I let him know that he should not be fearful about what he saw; I added that visions are messages from God to give to someone and that he was supposed to inform me that what I had could kill me. I would cease to be on this Earth if I did not listen to my son's message and heed the warning.

As Christians, we know the next step after death is eternity with our Father, so why are we so fearful of letting go of this temporal world of flesh for the exchange of spiritual life in Heaven? I was a scared Norton!

(Reference to The Honeymooners, circa 1955-1956) It was weird; on that same Tuesday night, I felt ok. But after my son's vision had the opportunity to sink in, I was horrified, becoming so numb that my mind went blank. Death knocked on my door, and I was *not* eager to open it. Therefore, I put my "brave face" on that Wednesday morning and was off to work as usual. The most significant difference now is that I went in each subsequent day feeling worse than the previous one.

My job was a half-hour away in Ballantyne, an affluent section of South Charlotte. I was the Desktop Support Lead at the site. My office was closed off to the rest of the employees, and I did most of my duties from my desk - which helped tremendously because I was becoming too weak to go on the floor.

I would struggle to get to work, rest for about an hour and a half, regain enough strength by noon to finish the day off, then drive home and hit the bed…HARD! Yet

Friday, August 19, 2016, was unique. Yes, I still struggled all day, and that 30-minute ride home felt like an eternity, but when I arrived home *this* day, all I could think about was Jaiden's ominous prediction. I was consumed with it. I went to lie down on my bed and began to cry. When Jaiden walked into the room to check on me, I quickly wiped my face and told him I was ok. I did not want to upset him – especially after (convincingly) calming him down.

Well, it might have worked with Jaiden, but that "I'm ok" story was ***not*** passing with my wife. Felicia had had enough. She said she was taking me to the ER. She was tired of the boys seeing their dad come home every night, go straight to bed, and not interact with them. Felicia asked Hannah to watch the boys while she took me to the emergency room, not knowing what we were about to come up against.

CHAPTER 3
ER

For nothing will be impossible with God.
                                    Luke 1:37

God can do anything but fail. That is huge! It means God can fix it - no matter *what* you go through. And even being privy to that divine knowledge, unfortunately, most of us remain "tangible" beings who must touch and see things to believe in them. But God! At one point or another, He has allowed us to see something incredibly inexplainable. I urge you to meditate and think back over your life; you will see something seemingly impossible that God has done for you or someone you know (clouds of witnesses – Hebrews 12).

Sometimes the decisions we make – be it under pressure or well thought out, can be critical. Merely deciding to go left or right can result in a life-changing event. When Felicia asked me, "Which emergency room do you want to go to, Presbyterian Matthews or Presbyterian Main?" I said, "Matthews." I felt terrible; I wanted to get to whichever was the fastest route.

Thinking about it now, in retrospect, I subconsciously chose the one in Matthews because Main is where Matt died. I am under the belief that God suggests options to us. Spirit to spirit. Not that I doubt they would have taken good care of me at Main, but I guess God whispered to me to go to the other facility. We listen to the voice we are familiar with. If we know what God's voice sounds like, we listen; if not, we ignore it.

Another example of that happening to me occurred one night back in 1989. I was hanging out at my girlfriend's place about 20 minutes from my apartment in Baisley. I was about to go home, but she asked me to stay longer. Get your mind out of the gutter! We were new in our relationship, and we loved spending time together.

Anyway, I would usually leave at a specific time because it was getting late, and I relied on public transportation back then. I believe her *"inner voice"* told her to ask me to stay later. At that moment, I had the option to either remain a while longer or go home. That inner voice told me to stay too, so I listened. It was an extra hour before I made it to the bus stop. As I waited, a Dollar Van approached. I liked taking the vans because they were quicker than the buses.

Fifteen minutes later, the van arrived near my apartment. It was at the traffic light, so I told the driver I would get out while he was stopped. As I walked in the direction of my building, I saw police cars. My sister was peering out one of our windows, waiting for me. I went towards her, and she quietly told me to use the back staircase. Then she said, "Someone killed Dewny!" Her words shocked me - not because Dewny was a few years younger than me, but if I had left my girlfriend's home just one hour earlier, I could have been lying in a pool of blood.

God is that *inner voice* that directs us. He will tell us when to go left instead of right. Like when He spoke to my former coworker as he waited for the elevator on the 13th floor of the World Trade Center on September 11, 2001. That inner voice said, "Go to the bathroom." And fortunately, he listened. The plane hit the building - completely severing the elevator shaft, causing it to fall to the ground killing everyone in it. My coworker emerged from the bathroom and was able to navigate down thirteen flights of stairs unharmed.

Sometimes we pay more attention to our flesh. We clearly hear God declare, "Go left," but in stubbornness or ignorance, we hang a right. And when our decisions bring about failure, we tend to blame God. *Then* we want to know why He did not save us from ourselves! This is not unlike watching our children and seeing ourselves in them. We have often warned them about potential dangers and have also been ignored. Like them, we must learn to talk to our "Father" to help us make the right choice. He only has our best interests at heart.

Talk to your Father daily, so you know that it is Him when you hear His voice talk to your inner voice.

Now, back to the trip to the hospital. We got to the emergency room in Matthews, NC, and they took me to the back. By then, I have two thoughts: 1. God gets me through everything; I will be home in a couple of hours, and 2. Jaiden's prophecy. If I go with the first, I am good to go. If I indulge in the second, I am dead. As I waited in the room, I was so out of it that I just wanted to be seen and to get this trip to the ER over with.

Felicia is a "rough love" person. She expresses her love for me differently – through *acts of service*. What I mean by that is she does not get overly affectionate with me – she is not the warm, fuzzy, huggy type of wife. There was no crying and waiting for things to happen around us at the hospital; my wife went to the desk to tell them what was happening to me like a pro. Our wait was brief, but during that short time, Felicia went to work! She immediately began texting our church family because she understood she needed all the help she could get. She also knew she did not want to do this family thing as a single parent. She needed to find out what was wrong with me and gather all the necessary resources to keep us healthy and together. She was a "rock" for the entirety of my illness. She went to work, ensuring we were good, cared for the house, cooked, and cleaned. I know I left out something; oh yeah, and all while still serving in her ministries at church.

Another one of my pet peeves is when people say, "I don't need to *go* to church, or I can do church in my home." We often make excuses for refraining from church – "People are phony," "I'm not giving them my money," etc. Those may be factual statements, but it still gets under my skin. When folks speak things like that, indirectly, they are declaring they do not need anyone and can essentially do life alone. Maybe these people have not experienced life with help, but for me, life is much easier with my "church folk." Not perfect, easier. The unity is undeniable, and the way the church family sprang into action duration my illness solidifies my beliefs. Keep reading, and you will see why you should find a place of worship. My acknowledgments at the beginning of this book only show a fraction of my enduring gratitude for my church family.

Remember Life Group? I always get excited every February when Life Group season starts. We would never miss a Thursday night. Great food, great fellowship, insightful teachings, and great friendships but mostly great support! As I mentioned before, the concept of it is to break a large church into smaller groups. Small support groups = extended families. Felicia and I love the idea, and we joined one when we became members at New Beginnings.

I had been running from God, but I think I was tired because something felt right about New Beginnings and the Fords' Small Group. That is who Felicia texted when we were in the waiting room – our Life Group members. Min. Rose Ling and Min. Donteia King came out to the ER at 3 AM after their "Sister-in-Christ" Felicia texted them. God spoke; they listened and came out to support us.

> *Everyone kept feeling a sense of awe, and many wonders and signs were taking place through the apostles. And all those who had believed were together and had all things in common; and they began selling their property and possessions and were sharing them with all, as anyone might have need. Day by day, continuing with one mind in the temple and breaking bread from house to house, they were taking their meals together with gladness and sincerity of heart, praising God and having favor with all the people. And the Lord was adding to their number day by day those who were being saved.*
>
> *Acts 2:43-47*

Life is built around family. Negative situations and thoughts occur when we gravitate to the family the *enemy* has sent instead of utilizing and embracing the family God plants around us. God knows we need help, and He provides us with the assets required to explore life fully. Things cannot move properly when we isolate ourselves from those He sent.

Back to the waiting room

One of the nurses came in and took my temperature and blood pressure. The phlebotomist comes in and is very proactive. I later found out that he served in the military. Instead of just taking my blood, he inserted a pick line for an I.V. – stating, "Just in case." After sending the blood specimens to the lab, he returned and informed me about how elevated my white blood count was. He said the level was 44 and looked like leukemia, but we had to wait to see what the doctor said. It was late, so we had to hang on until 7 am the following day. Thank

God for the church family. They came to us to support and comfort us in a time of the unknown and uncertainty. This helped us, for the moment, forget about the situation at hand.

Saturday, August 20, 2016, 7 AM: Dr. Newman confirms, "You have leukemia." I think I started to cry, Felicia put her arm around me, and she started crying. I did not focus on her previously elusive hug. All I could think of was Minister Matt, who passed in October 2015 from cancer, Minister Trent, who was just treated for cancer, and now me. All three of us were licensed together as Ministers in 2012.

God, what is going on? All I could think about was how Jaiden was right, I was going to the hospital, and I was going to die. I remembered hearing a sermon once, and the preacher talked about the "BUT" of God, and I was consumed with them… *But,* I have yet to live out my purpose! *But* why would God send me a message to prepare me for death? *But*, what about my wife and my children? Then, Dr. Newman had one of his own when he said, "You have leukemia, *BUT* many advances have been made towards a cure. We stopped crying and started listening. We heard death, *BUT* then we heard life. Dr. Newman said he wanted me to get the best treatment in the region, and we would have to travel to Wake Forest Baptist Hospital in Winston Salem, NC, to get it.

Without thinking or praying about anything, we agreed. We should have at *least* prayed about it, but we felt it was right. The prophecy was revealed through Jaiden's vision, so we already knew God placed us where we should be, but we were still nervous. With prophecy, there is always confirmation. God will send His people confirmation because He knows us. He knows that sometimes with prophecy comes a feeling of uncertainty, and (on occasion) we do not or will not move, but the confirmation is to calm us and *help* us move.

My sister Helen called me once she heard the news. We told her of the plans to move me to Winston Salem. Out of concern, she asked us if there were other options. And to be honest, through all the mayhem of the day, I cannot remember if we ever asked. Helen said, "Take the ride up and see what they have to say." Few words, but enough to serve as confirmation to go.

Life can be noisy and complex. Sometimes, we must isolate ourselves from the noise to hear God and the people He sends us. I had to be able to hear Felicia and her plea for my life to get me to move from my bed to the emergency room. It was a push that ultimately led me to an accurate diagnosis of Leukemia AML, the right doctors and nurses for care, and my ability to share my story with you.

Before I left for Winston-Salem, I gave my wife the assignment to field all calls and answer any questions.

The only thing I could do now was to wait for my

ambulance ride.

CHAPTER 4
Road Trip

*And the Lord appointed a great fish to swallow Jonah, and
Jonah was in the stomach of the fish three days and three nights.*

Jonah 1:17

God wanted Jonah to go to Nineveh. Jonah did
not want to follow God's plan, so he fled to Tarshish
instead. Like Jonah, we tend to run from God's
assignments for different reasons or excuses, but mainly
because we allow our flesh to dictate our life's purpose.
But God knows how to get us where we need to be - even
if He uses a "big fish" or a particular situation to get us
there.

My mind was all over the map while waiting for
the ambulance. I felt like I was traveling too far away
from my family, not knowing if I would return. You have
to understand that, even though I am a believer, I still live

in this flesh, and (in times of distress) there is a constant struggle – good versus evil, right versus wrong. The following verse gives biblical insight:

> *So then, on the one hand, I myself, with my mind, am serving the law of God, but on the other, with my flesh, the law of sin.*
>
> *Romans 7:25b*

One issue with Christians is that we testify to the victory but neglect to acknowledge the struggle fully. I often wanted God to take my "cup," my work - not wanting to do it as I was going through it. But as God walks us through the struggle, the burden is lessened. We must embrace what God is allowing to happen to us. The one thing I knew was that God did not *give* me leukemia; he *allowed* me to partake in a challenge.

When the ambulance arrived, two EMT workers emerged with a stretcher to gather me and my belongings. I wish I could remember their names because they performed their duties with excellence. Felicia said she had to take care of some things at home, and she would drive up to the hospital directly afterward. The EMT workers rolled and lifted me into the ambulance as I said goodbye to Felicia.

Habitually, I refrain from long drives. To compensate for the times that they are unavoidable, I listen to music, have a conversation with whoever is in the car, or do some FaceTime shenanigans. On this night, there was no music in the ambulance. No talks with the drivers – they were in the cabin, and my Facebook Live operator (Felicia) was not with me. I had to find something to occupy my (almost) hour and a half ride, so I prayed. I asked God, "What do you need me to do?" That was all I inquired of Him. I realized I was on assignment – that there was a purpose for this. And I also knew that things do not happen without reason. God answered me with SILENCE! Folks say, "Silence is golden," but just then, I needed Him to talk to me! I wanted to hear His voice. I cannot remember my thoughts for the rest of the ride, but for now, I will reflect on my father, mother-in-love, and my brother. All of whom have gone to Glory.

Back in the '90s, Pop was diagnosed with throat cancer. He used to smoke heavily, but when he was diagnosed, he stopped smoking. They were able to get rid of his cancer with laser surgery, but it reemerged, and this time it aggressively spread throughout his body. Strangely enough, sadness did not overwhelm the family. From my perspective, we all seemed to be at peace. I was almost in a fog. I went to visit Pop in the hospital. We probably talked about the Yankees (our favorite team). But I remember he had a smile on his face like he was proud. And I was pleased with the visit because that is all I wanted…quality time with him and a feeling of approval. I guess that is what most children may wish – for their fathers to be proud of them. Pop never said it, but I always knew that he loved me.

When one of my sisters visited him, she told me that she heard him talking to someone in his room. When she entered his room, there was no one there. I think he was having a conversation with an angel. I wondered if my father accepted Jesus as Lord and Savior and if I would one day see Pop in heaven. After she told me about her visit with him, I believed.

There are two things that I am fully *"anti"* – cigarettes and illegal drugs, i.e., marijuana, heroin, crack, etc.... Felicia's mother once asked me to pick up a pack of cigarettes from the store. I told her, "Ma, cigarettes killed my dad, and I am not going to the store to pick up something that will contribute to killing you." She was upset with me, but I could not partake in an activity that could harm someone I love.

Concurrently, I have seen how illegal drugs have destroyed communities and people. They can turn buildings and their inhabitants into mere shells of what and who they were intended to be. More importantly, I have witnessed how they can take away someone you love too soon, like the one I wish I could have spent more time with - my brother, Ralph Jr., aka Bubba.

Bubba liked to have a good time with the family but was very serious when he needed to be. When I was young, I often traveled to his high school with my mother because he would get into trouble. My mother told me we went to his school so much that they thought I was a student! I was blind to it then, but Bubba was using drugs, and my parents did a great job shielding his addiction from me. When it comes to family, I always want to know what the deal is – whether good, bad, or indifferent; I want to know. Yet it seems that with anything that had to do with Bubba, I was always "a day late and a dollar short" on the information.

After high school, Bubba eventually enlisted in the Army, got married, was stationed in Germany, and had a son. He served four years and moved back to the states. I cannot recall the exact year, but I remember visiting him at a rehab facility. And as late news would have it, it was only on the ride back from that visit that I learned Bubba was HIV positive, but actually, he had full-blown AIDS. When I found out he was full-blown – it was time to say goodbye.

I am not blaming anyone, but my time with my brother felt like it was cut short. I did not spend nearly as much time as I wanted with him. I knew he had an illness and should have reached out more. But as I reflect, was it necessary to know about his health to reach out to him and spend time? The answer is NO. We should reach out more to others regardless of their circumstances and live life with purpose *on* purpose. The more urgent the condition, the more urgent the purpose. It is a tragedy to have the last memory of a loved one to be in the hospital, wracked with pain, with sores all over their body. Regrettably, that was

how my last meeting with Bubba occurred at Brookdale
Hospital in Brooklyn, NY.

It was Christmas 1994. My brother Glenn, who
was in town, and a bunch of the family went to visit
Bubba. I was happy we could all visit him, but unlike the
last days with Pop, the overall mood this time was solemn.
The week following the visit went quickly. On Friday,
December 30th of that year, I came home from work
exhausted and took a nap. That was unusual for me. On
the rare occasion that I *did* nap, I would not dream, but it
happened this time. I was in a treehouse, and a soldier was
present. I turned to him, and he said, "Don't worry, he is
ok." Just then, I was awakened by my phone ringing. It
was my sister Helen, and she said, "Bubba passed."

*Were all these thoughts (of loved ones who have passed) the
enemy invading my headspace on the way to the hospital?*

As the ambulance pulled up to Wake Forest
Baptist Health, I did not want to be there; the only thing

my flesh had me focused on was death. It can be so depressing, plus God never answered my question, "What do you need me to do?" Then it hit me. God has *always* been there for me, even when I was out of position with Him. He has been directing me all my life. Everything I have gone through was instructions for the next steps of my journey. Now I could hear Him clearly. I was to encourage. He instructed me to "Encourage all those who come in your presence." That blew my mind. Here I am with a death sentence over my life, and I am to inspire those who heal. Death arrived to soothe the healers - not physically but spiritually.

Oh-oh, we are about to have some fun...

What we see with our mortal eyes as bad situations, God has a plan to turn them around. We need to open our hearts and allow God to speak to us and open our ears to hear what God is saying to us. When we focus on our assignment, He will do mighty works through us!

CHAPTER 5
Wake Forrest Love

Love is patient, love is kind and is not jealous; love does not brag and is not arrogant, does not act unbecomingly; it does not seek its own, is not provoked, does not take into account a wrong suffered, does not rejoice in unrighteousness, but rejoices with the truth; bears all things, believes all things, hopes all things, endures all things.

1 Corinthians 13:4-7

Anthony Davis   •••

August 22, 2016 (posted)

The past 4 weeks has been challenging with my health. At first thinking that I was dehydrated, to being told I had a sinus infection, to finding out this past Friday that my white blood cells were extremely high. So the doctors have determined that I have leukemia. I will have a bone marrow test today to determine what stage it is at.

I just wanted to send my FB family a word of encouragement. This is the beginning of my testimony - the testing stage. Yes, I am nervous. Yes, I am scared. But God! I could easily ask God to "take this cup" but God has entrusted me with this challenge.

Just remember, God causes all things (good, bad, indifferent) to work together for good to those who love God, to those who are called according to His purpose.

My purpose isn't over and neither is yours. Live out your God given purpose.

Be Blessed!

It can be easy to tell someone, "I love you." Three simple words that can make another person feel special. But these words, as fulfilling as they are, can sometimes be empty. For love is an action word. Saying love is the first step but showing love completes the action. Love is also obedience.

God assigns us people to love on – especially during times of despair. As Christians, we love and serve from obedience and sometimes because we feel it needs to be done. I am not saying that we should not instinctively love or serve, but before completing any assignment we feel we hear from God, we need to pause and ask, "God, do you *need* me there?" Do not go because of convenience or because you are concerned about what people will or will not say. God does not always need us "on site." Sometimes, He just wants us to talk to Him about the situation.

I never thought any less of anyone who did not visit me. Being hospitalized over an hour from where I live was a good thing. I was far enough away to where people had to give pause before heading out. If I were in Charlotte, my room would have been constantly flooded, and as part of my assignment from God, I needed to be isolated. I had to be in a position to be blessed *and* to be a blessing. God needed me to do ministry, and how could I minister to the doctors, nurses, patients, and people who loved me (both near and far) if my room was overpopulated? So, when it comes to showing me love, I equally thank everyone who drove up and those who did not because they were obedient to God *and* their purpose.

Some may find my following comment controversial, but just because a deed is good does not mean it is from God. For example, helping an old lady across the street is an excellent gesture, but it can be terrible if the light is red, and traffic is flowing while you are doing it. In other words, before you do your kind acts, ensure it is in line with what God calls you to do.

My journey in life has allowed me to cross paths with great people and some not-so-great. I always try to do what my parents taught me, "Treat people the way you want to be treated." The one thing I know I am capable of is treating people well. Being nice does not rob you of anything; there is no monetary cost - it just expands who you are. And I guess my friendly character and love towards others were mirrored during my stay in the hospital. I never realized how much people loved me, but I believe God gave me a preview before the actual "movie release" of my illness.

I had been training to be a Minister since November 2009 and preparing for graduation in 2012. Near completion of the course, my sister informed me that one of my friends I grew up with (Van) was trying to get in touch with me. I phoned him, and he said that he and

Todd (another childhood friend) would come down from New York for the graduation. We had not spoken to each other in almost 20 years, and they were not trying to get money from me. They traveled that far to support their brother without any ulterior motives…that was love—and only a tiny glimpse of what was to come.

If you recall, I mentioned that when I was diagnosed with Leukemia, Felicia did not keep silent; she reached out to family and friends. And I suggest to any spouse or caregiver not to take on life changes concerning your spouse or family members on your own. These challenges are not meant to be taken on in solitude; use your community. I am still trying to figure out why people hide situations when they need help. The moment you are going through something, and your "spirit-man" is sharing space with your "flesh-man," the principles are difficult to apply. LOOK, I was about to go through the battle of my life! Why would I want to be silent? Why would I want to hide it? If you were in a burning building, would you be quiet or scream, "HELP!"

Sometimes we get it backward by speaking when we need to be silent and then silent when we need to talk. I am grateful that my family got it in the correct order. During my battle, the three most essential things occurred: • Jaiden saw the smoke (his vision) • Felicia drove me to the ER (for a diagnosis), and I obeyed (agreed to be treated). They saved my life. In other words, having God's Word through His messengers is good, but you need *all things* from God to get you through. They did what you do when a "fire" is present – told someone and got help. If Jaiden did not react to the vision, if Felicia had not taken me to the hospital, and if I continued to lay in bed, I might not be alive today.

The only thing close to "near death" is death itself. If we are not dead, we have a purpose. If we have a purpose, then God is not through with us.

As believers, we are supposed to rely on God, and because I was about to go through something I had never experienced in my body, I needed to trust entirely in Him and what He was about to do through me. It was also necessary to acknowledge *who* He had sent to me.

When we go to church, we hear God's message delivered through God's messenger, and then we are to take these messages and apply them to our lives. It should be simple, right? Yes, but often our spirit and our flesh are in constant flux. One desires to do God's purpose, and the other does not. Like living with a roommate, you have to get up early, and your roommate wants to party all night. The Spirit of better judgment tells the roommate, "Party over," but the flesh says, "Party over here!" The latter being an outcome that will *not* work for your good.

We must get away from the voices that do not belong to God. Those voices are only there to confuse and distract you from His purpose for your life. I could have easily given up, but I knew God was not done with me. How did I know? I heard God's voice, listened, and responded. God is always speaking, but we tend to muffle it when it does not align with what we want to do. Never ignore your weaknesses! They are there to remind you of how much you need God's help. Listen to God, respond with all your available strength, and He will help with your weaknesses.

Everyone has God-given talents. Sometimes they are revealed to us by people in our circle. My gifts are *faith* and *exhortation*, a fancy way of saying I am an encourager. Kevin, a friend from church, disclosed the latter to me in conversation. He said, "You know you have the gift of exhortation." I never realized it until then, but I now notice that when I am around someone operating in *their* gifts, I love exalting them and watching them grow. I am just as excited as they are - despite any personal distress I may be going through. And regarding my faith, these days, it does not dissipate; it has gotten so powerful that I am in a constant state of expectation. In full transparency, I was not always that way, but the more I exercised my faith, the stronger it became.

One tricky thing about a gift is that although you love to give it, it might be a rarity to receive it back. This can be exhausting! In my case, God wanted me to encourage those who entered my hospital room. I would be tired from the chemotherapy treatments and still encouraging God's people. It would wipe me out. So, what did God do? He sent the right people to encourage, love on me, and fill me back up so I could continue my assignment.

CHAPTER 6
Wake Forest Seeding

"Go and say to Hezekiah, 'Thus says the Lord, the God of your father David, "I have heard your prayer, I have seen your tears; behold, I will add fifteen years to your life.

Isaiah 38:5

So many employers are moving away from autonomy and gravitating towards group results. They have found this model profitable, and the actual *team* unit is the key to any successful project or assignment. You can be the lead/head of the assignment, but it would be difficult to complete without the other members. Each person on the project must follow their objective within the work – usually, an area they are gifted in, and if they perform outside of their wheelhouse, the project could fail.

On Monday, September 5, 2016, I received a special visit...my friend Troy and his wife! Troy and I used to work together. It was one of the most enjoyable times in my employment history. He is a Reverend at Silver Mount Baptist Church, and every day at 4 PM, after a hard day's work, we would talk Bible. We always engaged in raw, honest, and entertainment-filled conversations about ministry, family, and church. Our discussions would take biblical characters and transform

their stories into a present-day, relatable format, like
turning a story like this:

> *Then Joseph had a dream, and when he told it to his brothers, they hated him even more. He said to them, "Please listen to this dream which I have had; for behold, we were binding sheaves in the field, and lo, my sheaf rose up and also stood erect; and behold, your sheaves gathered around and bowed down to my sheaf." Then his brothers said to him, "Are you actually going to reign over us? Or are you really going to rule over us?" So, they hated him even more for his dreams and for his words.*
>
> *Genesis 37:5-8*

Into this:

While his brothers toiled in the field, Joseph, the youngest son, tells his brothers about a dream he had. He tells them, "One day, I am going to have a huge corporation, I will be your boss, and you will all be tasked with cleaning my building." And his brother Reuben said, "Ninja, What?!" "Boy, you better step away from me with all that mess!"

Joseph's dream sounded like trash-talking, which annoyed his older siblings. He probably did a ton of other "little brother" stuff too, i.e., chatting non-stop, tattling, always hanging close to his parents - who seemed to favor him over the others, and just being an overall pain in the neck. One day, his overworked brothers took a small break from their duties. Joseph immediately rats them out to their dad, saying they are slacking at their responsibilities. His annoying tendencies and what they perceived as nonsensical dreams made the brothers dread his presence even more. You see, we would retell the story without losing the gist of the scripture!

Everyone does not easily digest the Bible, but by making the stories applicable to the things we experience today, people are more apt to listen, understand, and want to engage in the Word.

Every conversation that I have with Troy starts innocently enough but ends with an important message. The fact that he and his wife drove close to two hours to see me in the hospital spoke volumes about our relationship as "brothers" in Christ and his obedience to God's voice. When God spoke, Troy responded.

I believe God wanted me away from Charlotte, so I was not overly accessible to everyone. There are times that we minister when God does not want us to – we exercise our free will for the good of humanity, and it still qualifies as an act of love, but it is out of His assignment for us at that time. That is why, whenever I give my testimony, I thank people for their obedience through their prayers, love, thoughts, or for doing nothing. When God places a name on your heart, act; if He says nothing, do nothing. Doing nothing does not mean you refuse to show your love and kindness; it means to be still for that moment. When I saw Troy walk in, I knew we would have a great conversation, but I was also excited about the sermon I would hear. God sent Troy on *this* day to give me a message concerning Isaiah 38:1-5.

Troy and his wife sat down, we exchanged
pleasantries, caught up with each other, and then he got
right down to business. He reminded me of King
Hezekiah and how Isaiah came to him and gave him a
message from God that he would die. And how Hezekiah
prayed to God, and his life was extended. Then Troy told
me, "God is not finished with you. He trusts who you will
give all the glory to." Then Troy stood up, walked around,
looked at the room, and said, "It is good, it is good here."
After he was finished, I looked at him and said, "When
you started, I was nervous. I thought God was sending you
here to tell me I was going to die."

In times like those, we need to pay *close* attention. We need to really listen to the messengers that God sends us. The second part of the scripture states that years were added to Hezekiah's life! Things we go through are more prominent than us, and the assignments seem even more significant. But God. God trusts us. These assignments are significant, and an audience must be reached for each. Someone did their mission to get us where we are today. We are all in this together; Paul plants, Apollos waters, but God provides the increase. Do your part so God can do His.

CHAPTER 7
Wake Forest Watering

"And they will fight against you, but they will not overcome you, for I am with you to save you," declares the Lord."
Jeremiah 1:19

When I was younger, I used to be terrified of hospitals. If I had to visit family members, the conditions were not the greatest, the food seemed nasty, and often, it was the last time I saw them alive. Those reasons created fears in me that almost prevented me from getting healed. I eventually learned to replace my fears with faith. If I believed this was not the end, I had to be confident that I would leave this hospital alive. God created these doctors and nurses. I had to trust that God was working through them.

When I say I had an incredible staff, it is an understatement. From when I was rolled into the hospital until I left, they treated me like royalty. Never nasty, very patient (no pun intended), and when I was nervous about a procedure, they would take their time – step by step. At night, when they had to take my vitals, they would gently wake me up. All but one of my nurses were female; nurse Rodney was the exception. I remember when I met him for the first time. He said, "I am your nurse for tonight, Nurse Rodney." I told him, "I guess you don't get *any* respect." Crickets … not even the slightest smile.

Before I crack a joke, I check a person out. Rodney was an older white man, so I assumed that he had to be familiar with Rodney Dangerfield (you younger readers YouTube him). Rodney Dangerfield was a comedian whose tagline was. "I don't get no respect." Nurse Rodney's no sense of humor would be a good challenge for me, but Felicia was not digging him.

Nurse Rodney had a deep voice and was very soft-spoken. One night he woke me up to take my vitals. He said, "Anthony." I woke up and said, "Rodney, I thought that was God, and He was calling me home." He smiled and chuckled a bit, then proceeded to draw blood from my pick line. He was having an issue and went to get help. When he left, Felicia said, "I do *not* like him; let's get another nurse." I said, "No, let's give him a chance." Something about him felt right. I cannot explain it, but my discernment was not setting off any alarms. He returned with a phlebotomist who discovered that my pick line was not lined up correctly and that depending on how

I was laying, it would cut off the blood flow. The next day, they removed it and installed a new one.

Rodney was meticulous; he wanted to guarantee his patients received the utmost treatment. Later, I discovered his daughter had leukemia, and he was a widower. Rodney was also Christian…a true believer in Christ, and from then on, we began having great Biblical conversations. And (to think) we almost dismissed him because what we saw with our eyes was not pleasing to us. If we did not give him a chance, we might not have seen what was in his heart – the way God sees us all.

Why are we so quick to move in judgment? We are built differently and move at dissimilar paces. Sometimes life rewires us and makes us appear one way on the outside but creates a new being on the inside. Our God is like a crockpot. No matter who we are, He takes His time with us to "soften" us. We (on the other hand) are so quick to eat the meat that we do not have the patience to ensure we cook it through to tenderness. If I had not waited on God to show me Rodney's heart, I would have never been able to fellowship with him. Rodney, it was a pleasure to be in your presence.

From Nurse Sharie to Ciara ("Ciara in the house") and all the nurses worldwide, God Bless You!!! I will tell you what I told my nurses. You did not give me leukemia, so I cannot be mad at you. Some patients have difficulty viewing it that way. They are angry because they are displaced from home and familiar surroundings.

To all the nurses, *please* keep doing what you are called to do. We, your patients, are not perfect, and we need you to guide us back to health. My four weeks in Wake Forest Baptist felt like it was quick, and I attribute that to the staff that God placed me under. People might say I am over-spiritualizing things, but I see it differently. What should have been painful was not, and what should have been depressing was joyful (ok, maybe the meds are talking now), but I honestly think that when we listen to God's voice and follow His direction, everything moves in His time – quickly.

Because of my previously discussed aversion to long-distance driving, I disliked the time Felicia and I had to drive to Miami for our friends' (Vinnie and Sharon) wedding renewal. Vinnie asked me to perform their ceremony, and we could not afford to fly. Aside from that, we had to take (a 10yr old) Jaiden with us. Even though I dreaded the drive, being there for our friends was more important than my distaste for the mode of travel.

To combat my loathing of these extended drives years ago, I figured if I could envision myself at the end of the trip, the trip would go quickly. When I focus on the entirety of the journey, I count every second of every minute – making the ride torturous. How I manage to survive these excursions now is at the start of the trip, I look to the left of the highway and imagine myself already riding back.

Leukemia was like one of those arduous drives. At the beginning of my healing process, Dr. Powell told me I would be at Wake Forest Baptist for approximately four weeks. I had to recognize what God was showing me. I knew I would be healed, and according to Dr. Powell, I knew it would be four weeks, so I focused on that – the conclusion of my stay and God's Vision. Doing that made my time in the hospital fly by. When we focus on the process (man's time), it seems to go slowly. It seems to go quickly when we focus on the vision (God's time).

CHAPTER 8
The Port

But Moses said to the people, "Do not fear! Stand by and see the salvation of the Lord, which He will perform for you today; for the Egyptians whom you have seen today, you will never see them again, ever. The Lord will fight for you while you keep silent."

Exodus 14:13-14

The Israelites were escaping from Pharaoh's army, so Moses decided to give them a holy pep talk. He told them not to fear - even though he was scared. God told Moses to cross this vast sea, but Moses could not visualize it. There were no boats nor a bridge. How was he supposed to get these people across this vast obstacle? God told him to go forward, raise his staff, and get to the other side.

Why do we hesitate when God gives us simple instructions? God knows what we are capable of, so He knows what He needs to fulfill.

I had a softball game one Saturday morning and was playing left field. My friend Marc was playing left-center field. Stan, our catcher, knew most of the hitters in the league and instructed Marc and me to shift even *further* to our left. I moved, but Marc stayed put. I asked him why he ignored Stan, and when referencing the guy at bat, he said, "This guy always hits over here." I told him, "If he hits it away from where Stan told us to go, it's on Stan, but if he hits away from where we go, it's on us!" Stan (not only) knew the hitter but also where the pitcher would pitch the ball. Stan was giving us an advantage in the field. He was trying to make our job a little easier. God knows what happens. He also knows our strengths and weaknesses. We may not immediately be able to visualize what God wants us to do; trust Him. He knows the outcome.

As a precursor to chemotherapy treatments, I had

to get a port installed. The doctors explained the

procedure to me. I understood what needed to be done,

but I was still scared. It was a Tuesday, September 27,

2016, a doctor had never cut me before this date, and my nerves were on level 10! I remember that day well because it fell on my sister Ann's birthday.

Was it a coincidence that the procedure was on

my sister's birthday, or did God purposely orchestrate it

that way? I believe the latter. After the port procedure, I

decided to make Ann's special day my focal point for the

ride home by calling her and wishing her a happy birthday. It may sound silly, but I believe God gives us things to distract us so we can focus on the other side - the vision, not these large walls to our left and right.

They had to put me under local anesthesia to have the port installed. My technicians were great. My questions gave away my nervousness because they patiently walked me through the procedure. It was freezing in the room, so I could only think about the COLD. They had me lay on my side and told me they had to inject a needle into my neck to numb the area. They explained to me that it would feel like a bee sting, and it did. To further distract me, one of the techs told me to look at the blood pressure monitor and count down from ten, and strangely, I had complete trust.

Ten, nine, eight … I smell bacon… I heard a voice, "Mr. Davis." I sat up and felt foggy AND hungry. I had not eaten all day, and it was 6 pm. They gave me chips and soda to quell my pangs. I looked to my left, and it appeared as if they were laughing at me. I thought I was out of it for about five minutes…max, but when I went to the waiting room, Felicia told me that the process took two hours! That moment reminded me again of God's time versus ours. As quick as it started, it was over. My doctor said I was cleared to go, but we had to tell people to do "fist bumps" so they would not hurt my neck.

On the ride home, I called my sister, "Happy Birthday, Ann!!!" My neck was going to be sore, but I was on cloud nine - ready to celebrate this next step to recovery. I wanted to share it with my church family and was excited to see people there that I had not seen in months. This would be my first time at church since Jaiden's vision.

I remember when Matt came back to church after his

procedure. His was much more severe as he had an

Pictured: William "Matt"

operation to remove a brain tumor. Matt was my

inspiration. He worshiped like no other when he returned

to church after his procedure. He was pacing back and

forth, glorifying God. All eyes were on him, and Felicia

asked me to get him to sit down and rest, but I was

conflicted. I knew Matt - he was an outward "praiser," so

I did not want to stop him even though I knew he needed

his rest; I also did not think Matt would listen if I asked

him to sit and take it easy. I waited for the right time, hugged Matt, and whispered in his ear, "Let's sit down," and he did. After service was over, I walked with Matt to make his rounds as he greeted folks in the congregation. I felt like his personal armor bearer. I think Tangie and Felicia wanted me to walk with him to keep an eye on him.

Matt's time with us after his operation was very courageous. I learned how to respond when adversity struck by observing him. When God submits your name to the enemy, how do you respond? Do you get in the ring and give it everything you have and praise your Creator, or do you throw in the towel? I thank God daily for allowing Matt to be such an enormous part of my life for what turned out to be a brief time.

We can avoid attention like Moses and Jonah, but God always gets us where He needs us.

When it was my turn to return to church, Felicia and I entered through the Ministry Center - where our youth meet to worship. It was less crowded than the larger main entrance, and we wanted to attract the least attention going inside. But of course, God makes His plan, which *always* supersedes ours. Here we were…trying to sidestep attention, and God put us right smack in the middle of it. We chose a walk that would typically take 2-minutes to get to the main sanctuary, but it took us 15 minutes because every person we saw stopped and conversed with us.

We never realize how much it affects people when we go through tribulations until we see and hear about it for ourselves. These church members blessed me with love and words of encouragement, and in reciprocity, my initial victory inspired them. There was a purpose for what I was going through. To think that we inhabit the earth only to wake up, go to work, come home, and pay bills would be ludicrous. We have to be here for a bigger

purpose. I may be here for one individual, and that person

may be here for millions. But our ultimate goal is to help

another one of God's children, so *never* minimize your

purpose.

CHAPTER 9
The Treatments

But David said to the Philistine, "You come to me with a sword, a spear, and a saber, but I come to you in the name of the Lord of armies, the God of the armies of Israel, whom you have defied. This day the Lord will hand you over to me, and I will strike you and remove your head from you. Then I will give the dead bodies of the army of the Philistines this day to the birds of the sky and the wild animals of the earth, so that all the earth may know that there is a God in Israel, and that this entire assembly may know that the Lord does not save by sword or by spear; for the battle is the Lord's, and He will hand you over to us!"

1 Samuel 17:45-47

I did not acknowledge it earlier, but this is a three-part story. Part one was my sickness, two was my treatment at Wake Forest Baptist, and the third was my port installation. God had His hands all *in* it. As God guides us, He is training us for our "Goliath" fight - that one giant that we all eventually face in our life. He does it by exercising our faith-building and muscle memory so that we know when to bob, weave, duck, and counter. This way, we are prepared to react when the enemy approaches. He involved so many people in my "fight" that I could *feel* His presence.

When I say I love my wife, it is an understatement. Did I mention that before? Felicia has been tremendous! She was my in-hospital roommate: when I woke up, she was there. She was there when I needed an advocate, a cheerleader, or any type of assistance. Just like at the ER, she accomplished all those tasks while ensuring everything was okay at home and school; the boys were taken care of, the bills were paid, everyone in our circle was updated, and our jobs were secure. I know I am leaving something out, but you get the gist (I am trying to have her write a book… "Caregiving 101 – A Spouse's Guide Through Sickness and In Health").

During chemotherapy, things began to change.

There was a sudden instability. Felicia was back to work

and could not stay with me like before. I compare it to

Felicia Davis is 😴 feeling sleepy   •••
with **Anthony Davis**
at **WFBMC Comprehensive Cancer Center**
October 11, 2016 (posted)

Well we are back here in Winston Salem for 6 days of chemotherapy for **Anthony Davis**. Thanking God in advance for our support system being connected to a GREAT church New Beginnings has blown my mind. We have a team of MOG (Men of God) holding up their brother ladder, taking off work to spend the night then the next person coming in the next day. **Paulus Ford Herbert Downing III Donnie Saunders** you guys are the REAL MVP!!!! **Keith King Teia Nichole King Vanessa Mitchell Griffith Dennis Griffith** thank you for opening up your homes & time to look after the boys for us & I would be remised if I left off my #1 support **Hannah Padgett** for looking after her brothers each time we have to make this trip out here. We love you ALL for loving us & riding this thing out we still have a long way to go but we are definite we will have THE VICTORY after this. **#teamDavis**

using training wheels, and

God was about to take one

wheel away. I would have

to remain at Wake Forest

for four days in October and

four days in November. The doctors were trying to move the bone marrow transplant up. Still, I refused to be in the hospital during our anniversary in November and especially not in December because of Jaiden's birthday. Plus, because of the surrounding holidays, I wanted us to be celebrating them as a family. My wife was determined to make sure someone was in the room with me - just in case I needed assistance while she was away, so she reached out to my friend Rev. Paulus.

Aside from our Life Group, he was also the leader of the Men's Ministry at the time. She asked him if he could contact some of the brothers at church to see if they could take turns staying with me in her absence. Fortunately, I had the confidence and faith of David and a Proverbs 31 woman as my bride. I knew I would not fall – even with one wheel missing. Sidebar – this is a benefit of going to church. To extend that comment a little further – it is why you should *serve* at church.

As previously noted, Felicia and I serve in multiple ministries at our church – including a Life Group. People may say, "That is too much church," but no one said a peep when I was doing worldly things. I played softball three to four times a week, got up at 6 am on Sundays to pick up my players for a doubleheader - which would end at noon, and stayed in the park until 7 pm, drinking and talking about nothing. I would not arrive home until 10 pm because I had to drop my players off; no one said *that* was too much. So, when I became a member of my church, I told Felicia, "If I could give the world my time and receive nothing in return, I could surely give God my time and talent and receive His Blessing." And here is the funny thing, God does not ask for the same time from us that the world does.

Our involvement in the church has allowed us to meet like-minded, God-praising, incredible people who love us and respond to the Lord's calling. Rev. Paulus, being one, responded to Felicia's request and proceeded to reach out to the Men's Ministry. He got three men who were friends of mine: himself, Herb, and Donnie. Felicia was proactive - basing my need on the last time I was in the hospital. She wanted her "Man of God" adequately taken care of.

On Tuesday, Felicia stayed the night, and everything went well. Wednesday, Donnie came up in the morning and stayed the night; Thursday, Herb came up in the morning, stayed the night; and Friday, Rev. Paulus came up in the morning and stayed until Felicia came up after work – each day went well. For the subsequent chemo treatment in November, I stayed alone. God was preparing me for the next stage... the bone marrow transplant; I had to do it alone. All training wheels off!

Now that chemo was over; the transplant was scheduled for January 2017. Once completed, I would have to stay in the hospital for three weeks; then live in an apartment

near the hospital, in Durham, NC, for three months.

In December - just before the transplant, we came

home to Charlotte to find a note attached to the door of

Felicia Davis   •••
December 4, 2016 (posted)

It just dawned on me that tomorrow is **Anthony Davis** LAST chemotherapy treatment before his bone marrow transplant in January. I guess the reason for me being so darn emotional this week is because he will be away for 3 months & I couldn't keep it together for 6 days. I'm happy knowing that out of those 3 months I get to be his caregiver for 2 of them in Durham. I thank God for bringing us to a great body of believers that support us, not a day goes by that I don't get a text or a call checking on me from my church family. Thank you **Jason Wilson K Hairston Wilson Dennis Griffith Vanessa Mitchell Griffith** & **Hannah Padgett** for looking after the boys for us. Kera even went with my daughter on yesterday to pick up a live Christmas tree that was donated to our family with ALL THE TRIMMINGS. We don't ask for help it's always the opposite so thank you guys. **#teamDavis** has a big support system & we don't take it for granted. And thank you **Marjorie Faustin** for taking my Jaiden to school this week I appreciate you so much 😊

the house we were renting.

We paid the rent on time,

but the owner was not

paying the mortgage. We

had a choice, ride it out and

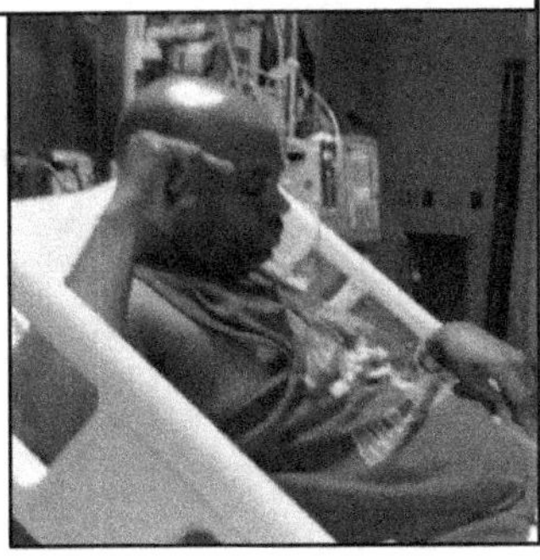

continue to pay or try and find a new place to live. We decided to relocate; we had to move swiftly.

We found a place and prequalified for it based on our income. Everything was going well until something popped up on my credit report. One of the places we used to live said we owed them approximately $300. We were denied. As I read the report, it showed that we settled for $300; therefore, making it paid. I talked to one of the representatives from the company, and she was fixated on page 3, where the charge was, but I also told her to read page 7. She did, and all she said was, "Oh."

Now, people who know me know that I use the following word either in love, jokingly, or in its pure definition for stupidity. I will let you figure out my intended meaning as I responded loudly (in my mind), "MEATHEAD!" By the time they finally listened to me, the house we wanted had been rented out.

There we were with less than two weeks to find, pack, and move to another place! This weighed heavily on me. I was about to live away from Charlotte for a quarter of a year. I needed to have my family secured in a home. I also needed this home to be a *clean* home for when I returned. I began to think about how when, shortly after I was born, our house was foreclosed, and we had to move to the projects. Not exactly what I consider clean living in today's world, and I could not fathom having my wife and kids live in that environment for *any* length of time.

I have always wanted to live in a two-story house. The funny thing is I did not consider the house we were leaving as a *real* home because it was a ranch. We looked for another two-story with the same company, but the rent was more than we wanted to pay, and Felicia became concerned. I told her we had no choice because our time was limited, and the rent was just enough where we would not get too comfortable. In other words, paying that rent rate would finally force us to purchase a house. With cleanliness being the benchmark, we chose the more expensive one.

God has been with us through this whole thing. Why would He desert us now? So we signed the lease, contacted our church family, and they had us moved out of the old and into the new place by Friday, January 6, 2017. Four days later, I was checked into Duke University Hospital, preparing for my bone marrow transplant. I thought that was one of God's biggest jokes on me. All the time, I teased my mother about not living in a house, and almost 50 years later, God let me live in a home…for *four* days! Let it be known that God *does* have a sense of humor.

CHAPTER 10
The Hardest Chapter

For I am convinced that neither death, nor life, nor angels, nor principalities, nor things present, nor things to come, nor powers, nor height, nor depth, nor any other created thing, will be able to separate us from the love of God, which is in Christ Jesus our Lord.

Romans 8:38-39

Paul, the author, is convinced that nothing, good or bad, can separate him from God's love. This was the second Bible verse I learned verbatim (the first being the Lord's Prayer). In the early '90s, I would listen to a John P. Kee song entitled, "I'll Serve Him," where he begins with the above verse. I loved the melody, so the verse stuck to my spirit.

*Do not let **anything** pull you away from God.*

It is one thing to deal with leukemia, but once I learned about having a bone marrow transplant, it became a different ball game. When I was first diagnosed, Felicia and I first thought about the mortality rate. We were also told about the deliverance; that is when we thought about the Kingdom and what God was getting ready to do in my life.

> *And He said, "Listen, all Judah and the inhabitants of Jerusalem and King Jehoshaphat thus says the Lord to you, 'Do not fear or be dismayed because of this great multitude, for the battle is not yours but God's.*
>
> *2 Chronicles 20:15*

God has a purpose for everyone, and what He wanted me to do was self-evident after my diagnosis. I knew he wanted me to do the Noah thing: tell my message until the flood. Simply put, get sick with a deadly disease, endure three weeks of chemo, have a port installed, do two more rounds of chemo, get a new port installed, and a bone marrow transplant, and on top of that, being away from my family for over two months. In a nutshell, that is what happened.

Even from the abridged version, one might ask, "Whew, how did you get through it?" Honestly, during this whole process, I kind of laughed through the pain., I was like, "WOW! God, you are incredible!" He made this process a breeze. Granted, there were times of pain, but they passed with the quickness.

Felicia Davis   •••
January 9, 2017 (posted)

We are so blessed with love from friends coming by to check on **Anthony Davis** before he heads to Raleigh in the morning. Thank you **Bro Clifton Morris Dennis Griffith James Ellison** for coming by today. My adopted parents The Ellison's came with dinner tonight. We love you all please keep our family lifted in prayer for these 3 months we already know the outcome.

The treatment at Wake Forest Baptist went so seamlessly that I believed the bone marrow transplant at Duke would also be a breeze. God was working on another one of His "too good to be true" type of plans, and I felt something was about to happen - like the enemy was looming around, waiting for me to drop my guard, discourage me, and break my spirit. The devil hates us, and he will do anything to stop us from fulfilling what

God has destined for us. He catches us when we are at our apex because the higher we are, the steeper the downfall, making it harder for us to get back up to the top of our peak of joy.

Before my trip to Duke, Felicia gathered our friends together for a celebration. She called it a "Re-Birthday" party. On my actual birthday in February, I was going to be in Durham, and when I received my new bone marrow from my brother Glenn, I would have a new blood type. It was like being born again. After the party ended, our daughter Hannah and Felicia argued. I am used to them fussing with each other, which was my norm. But it was a norm that I would not hear for the next couple of months. With all the dysfunction in our family, I still loved it. I had gotten so used to it that it became my personal reality show.

There was a "snowstorm" the weekend before my trip to Duke. I used quotation marks around that word because the ones down south differ from the ones in New York. Life closes for an inch of snow down here, which played a factor in my bone marrow story. When we arrived at Duke, it felt like a ghost town. A lot of employees were delayed because of the snow. That meant that everything for me was postponed to a later time, and I had a lot of tests that needed to be performed before being admitted. I also had to get a central line implanted - similar to my power port, except this one hung out of my chest. I called it "Kuato" (Google both, and you will get it).

We finally arrived on my hospital floor but found out that my original room was taken Most of the time, we

Felicia Davis is 🙁 feeling emotional   •••
with **Anthony Davis** at **Duke University Hospital**
January 10, 2017 (posted)

So the wife has checked the husband in his suite for the month LOL his nurses are very nice, showed us where the snacks were and the rules for his stay while here. I can't stay with him this time but will make my weekend visits before we move into our apartment for the 2 months in 3 weeks. I'm tired but had to make sure he was alright before heading back to Charlotte. Thanks for the prayers complain about being late. However, this time being late was a good thing.

We walked around the ward until we reached the last room, next to the emergency exit. The nurse told me I had the "penthouse"- the largest on the floor. Even though it was considered the penthouse, it was half the size of my room at Wake Forest Baptist.

Because of my experience at Wake Forest, I was not fearful at Duke, maybe a bit uneasy, but not overly alarmed. The staff at Duke was phenomenal. I was missing my roommate. I would have to ride this hospital stay primarily without Felicia. The first week was total preparation for the transplant. For about six days, I had to receive chemotherapy. They administered different "cocktails" – a combination of drugs to attack the cancer cells from different angles, and they were strong. The purpose of this chemo was to destroy my bone marrow so

I could receive my brother's bone marrow. On the seventh day – REST!

Most people think a bone marrow transplant is where they take the bone marrow from the donor's back and implant it into the patient. My brother, who was my donor, thought that was the procedure, but he was in for a surprise... six days of stomach shots!

I love my brother. We may not have expressed it verbally to each other, but we have always known and showed it. Well, Glenn stepped up BIG with this. I have never complained about the size of our family, but now I understand why so many of us were there. He took six shots for six days and said he would do it again. Glenn's seventh day was different from mine. He had to sit in a chair with a tube connected from his right arm to his left. While blood was leaving one arm on the way to the other, stem cells were extracted. And the next day, his stem cells were transplanted into me.

Being away from my family for the following 14 days was the most brutal. Felicia would only be able to come up on the weekend. The clock across from my bed was moving at a snail's pace. I mostly watched food and

Felicia Davis •••
January 25, 2017 (posted)

Day +7 **Anthony Davis** has had fever & chills throughout the day but never seems to amaze me with his continued strength. Never complaining about anything, always cheerful & encouraging me when I'm about to lose my mind (which is about everyday). His co-worker Vinny actually booked a hotel stay near the hospital & came back to spend the day with him again today. Thanking God for friends & family that's standing in prayer with us. Also for the cards that have came as well. If you want to send some encouraging words inbox me for his address. Be Blessed

home improvement shows (I was told it was the regular TV lineup for patients) to pass the time. My oncologist, Dr. Lopez, came in every morning with his staff. He would inform me of my progress and how amazed he was at how rapidly my numbers had increased each day. I knew why. I did not tell him then, but I was at peace. Regardless of the outcome, I had the victory if God allowed me to be healed – I had VICTORY! If God called me home to Him – it was still a VICTORY! Either way, there would be a party at the end.

I took this ailment seriously. God had me here for a reason. I never question Him. I had my "cup" moments when I would want God to take this burden from me, but those moments would be fleeting. I kept reminding myself: PURPOSE! What I was going through and going to get through was not for my glory; it was for *His*! And when this was all over, the non-believer would say, "God exists"; the backslider would say, "Prophecy and miracles are real"; and the true believer would say, "I told you so!"

I was anxious to get out of the hospital, and my numbers were excellent, but they usually will not discharge patients under three weeks after a bone marrow transplant. I was doing so well and had only seven days left. But the devil is crafty. He will do *any* and *everything* to get you to pull away from your assignment. I was in the hospital, excited and full of joy, ready to tell my story.

God already spoke to me about penning my book – I was prepared to start writing my testimony. He also prophesied through Pastor Henderson at the New Year's Eve service in front of the congregation that the doctors would speak of this miraculous recovery and how my book would touch many.

I was on cloud nine, full of joy, ready to boast to the world about what my God had done. Then came the night the enemy shook me, the night that put a pause to my purpose. It was Wednesday, February 1, 2017. I was in my room sleeping. The walls of the hospital rooms were not solid. They were the kinds separated with windows and blinds.

My blinds were open, so I could see my door and the room next door. Suddenly, I was awakened by a noise. I looked into my neighbor's room and saw this tall white man running out of his room to the right, down the hall. He could have easily run to the left and into my room or out the emergency door, but he did not, as if God was saying, "Don't touch my servant." This man appeared demon-possessed. He was there to strike fear and get me off my assignment, and temporarily, it worked. I got out of bed, pushed the tray against my door, closed the blinds, sat on the floor, and called security. Security said they were aware of the situation and had guards on the way up. I called Felicia, and she stayed on the phone with me until the nurses arrived in my room.

I later found out what happened. The nurses were in my neighbor's room doing their standard rounds when he jumped out of bed and ran from the room, leaving his IV behind and a trail of blood. While chasing one nurse, he stopped and redirected himself when he saw another wearing a cross on a chain necklace.

> *You believe that God is one. You do well; the demons also believe and shudder.*
>
> *James 2:18-20*

Not every patient on my floor had the strength to jump up and run out of their room. Even worse, we all had a central line connected and surgically installed. When my neighbor jumped up and ran out, he physically ripped himself from those connections – OUCH! The nurses went around the floor to check on everyone. When my nurse came to my room, she was visibly shaken. She had a look on her face like she had witnessed something she had never seen before. As we conversed, they were escorting my neighbor back to his room. It was akin to watching a horror movie; he looked like a zombie! And anyone who knows me knows that horror is not my film genre. I was extremely restless, and just as if I *had* seen a scary movie, I could not get to sleep that night. I felt unsafe in my flesh, but I knew my assignment was already confirmed in my spirit. God just allowed me to view spiritual warfare.

That was it for me. I could not stay there another day, let alone seven. I talked to Dr. Lopez and told him about my reservations. My numbers were good, my apartment was ready, and so was I. With everything conducive to proper healing, Dr. Lopez gave me the okay to leave, and I was discharged. This was the most challenging chapter. From beginning to end, I had to press

Anthony Davis
February 3, 2017 (posted)

Being discharged!!! Next stop our Durham apartment.

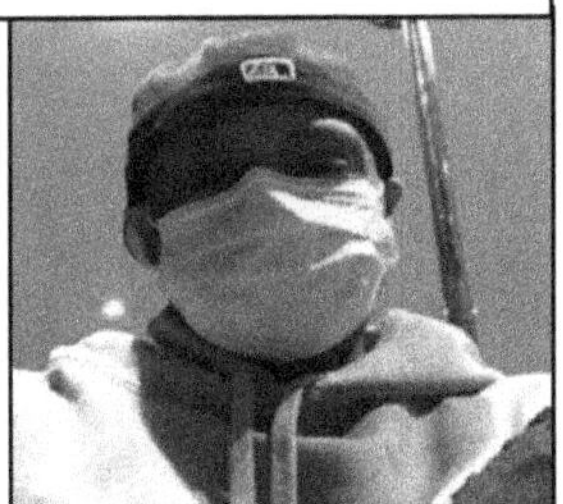

my way through. The next stop was the apartment for a couple of months—this time with Felicia and Jaiden.

CHAPTER 11
Outpatient

"Before I formed you in the womb I knew you, And before you were born I consecrated you; I have appointed you a prophet to the nations."

Jeremiah 1:5

Felicia Davis ···
February 3, 2017 (posted)

So our next journey starts today with Anthony being discharged from Duke University. When he first went in the doctors said he would be in the hospital for a month well that month hasn't come because he has been doing so well. Our next adventure is at our new apartment for 2 months with doctor visits everyday did I mention Sundays too? Today was my last day at work for 2 months so me & the boys will be headed to Durham where Jaiden will be going to school near the apartment a... See more

---

It was Friday, and Glenn picked me up to take me to the apartment. Thank You, Jesus! Each leg of this walk was different and challenging. Moving from the hospital to outpatient presented an entirely separate trial. I had to be close to the hospital for daily blood work and treatments. Most of the time, Felicia would take me to the clinic, but to give her a break, Glenn or my sister Kathy and my mother would fill in.

A bone marrow transplant is a complex process; it involves taking "baby steps" and being closely observed - first in the hospital and then as an outpatient. This was an amazing daily progression. My brother's bone marrow was now in my body! Since Glenn's bone marrow was foreign to my system, there was an internal fight. The bone marrow was trying to gain control, and my body was trying to reject it. That is why you first have to be in an apartment near the hospital; they need to observe how your body functions outside perfectly sterile conditions.

Long before Covid-19, I had to wear a mask whenever I left the apartment. The drive to the clinic was about 20 minutes. Before check-in, everyone who entered the building had to wash their hands and mask up. All the receptionists were great, but Shawn was my guy. Every day he was there, I would hear him say from across the room, "Good Morning, Mr. Davis!" He always had something pleasant to say, and sometimes at the desk, we would catch up on sports - especially March Madness. Afterward, I would sit in the waiting room until being called for lab work.

Generally, the wait was brief, no more than five minutes. Most times, Nurse Pearl or Nurse Patti would come for me and take my vitals – which was easy because I had that port ("Kuato"). I kept a positive attitude and tried to keep a fair amount of dialogue going, consuming my time there as much as possible with an upbeat attitude. I looked at it like this: they did this job for eight hours a day, five days a week, and everyone did not carry a similar demeanor as me. I am not being cocky in proclaiming that, just confident in what God was allowing to happen and what He would do. If my five minutes could make their day more enjoyable, so be it.

When the labs were finished, I would return to the waiting room before being escorted to the treatment area in the rear. The recliner I sat in was comfortable; Felicia sat in a chair beside me. We had access to snacks and ice (Felicia's fav). Once my labs were back, I would receive treatments for what I lacked. Magnesium was the worst – it felt like my feet were on fire ('nuff respect to my menopausal sisters).

Dr. Lopez or someone from his staff would then come and talk to me about my stats and how well I was doing. His teams were funny, and they would fight over me. Again, not to brag, but I was an easy patient. I remained optimistic, joked, and encouraged others. Yes, it was an arduous journey, but I could not let it stop me from finding the good in the process. The challenge was pulling people along with me and getting them to enjoy life through my "test." The immense satisfaction was watching the process unfold.

Sometimes, while we were waiting, we would hear some of the other patients' issues: • Blood clots in leg • 6 bags of magnesium • Having to walk on their heels • Graft versus host disease (GVHD) – a condition that might occur after an allogeneic transplant. In GvHD, the donated bone marrow or peripheral blood stem cells view the recipient's body as foreign, and the donated cells/bone marrow attack the body.

Each day I saw the same people, heard different stories, and saw different situations. My body responded positively, but other patients stayed the same or declined as I improved. This could be depressing because I was getting better, and they were not. I felt like I *had* to continue to fight for them; hopefully, through me, they could see that God was driving my fight. I would not give up. If I could touch just one person, and that one goes forward to inspire millions, who cares how it gets done – I just had to do it.

Hopefully, while reading this book, you are following the notes that Felicia posted throughout my illness. Believe it or not, people criticized it; I never understood why. People can be too critical of things for no apparent reason. What would you do in her situation…if you had a spouse who was dying? Would you keep silent or break down and release your thoughts? Would you have the tenacity to walk it out together and share what is happening with family, friends, and the world? I will never understand how Felicia's gift to post sustained my life and maybe someone else's. The posts allowed her not to be burdened by my sickness. She released the news of my diagnosis to people who could pray for me – corporately or alone. It also allowed people to reconnect with me and reconcile relationships.

In the infamous words of Mr. T, "I pity the fool." Yes, I pity those who continue to be tricked by the enemy and hold back the tribulations they are going through. I also pray for those who are not empathetic. If posts about people not doing well bother you, refrain from reading them. As for me and my house, we are grateful for the "serial poster" I call my wife. Keep posting, Fe! Sorry for my rant; I had to get it out. In its simplest form, a post can be a point of inspiration to get your mind off the dulls of life.

Felicia received a call from one of our friends, Min. Connie Harper, from church. She told Felicia that her nephew was diagnosed with leukemia and was flown by helicopter from Charlotte to Duke University. She said her nephew and his wife were a little down and asked Felicia if we could visit them. Felicia and I talked about it. She knew I would agree. Going through this stopped me from believing in coincidence and instead believing in purpose.

After one of my clinic visits, we walked to the hospital where her nephew, Eddie, was a patient. Although I believe in my purpose, I admit that the flesh was nervous. But I also knew that once I arrived, God was going to do His thing. I just had no clue *what* to expect from Him. It was like when I had to visit anyone I considered as being close to me in the hospital.

As ministers at New Beginnings Church, one of our assignments is being "Minister on Call" two to three times per year. You are *on-call* for a week and will be contacted with the names of people to call and pray with or visit (if they are in the hospital). About a month into being a full-fledged minister, one of my first calls was a visit to a gentleman in the hospital. He was not a church member, but we patronized his business. One day, after work, I went to visit him. I was extremely nervous. I did not know what to anticipate, and I had already expressed my disdain for hospitals. I got to his room, where he had a tracheotomy inserted in his neck and could not speak. Moreover, he did not understand English. I think he was Cambodian. All we were able to do was wave hello, give the nod to each other, say a little prayer, and then wave goodbye. Sometimes your presence is enough.

Our stay with Eddie was like this, but slightly different. Similar because it was a hospital visit. Different because Eddie and I were both dealing with leukemia and spoke English. We had a good visit with Eddie. His wife was there, and we tried to keep them uplifted. Felicia encouraged his wife from the caregiver's perspective, and I did my part to reassure Eddie from the patient's. Some of his family stopped by too, and with all of them present, Felicia and I simply opened our mouths and let God speak through us to all of them.

One thing I made it a priority to speak to Eddie about was ministry. I told him that God was not done with us, and we had a ministry to do together. Eddie was a believer – with a church home, so I knew he received what I was saying. We understood that we had to be strong for those who do not believe and show God's love through our pain. As God works through us, people are delivered to Him. About a month later, Eddie passed.

The hardest thing about this journey was watching people suffer and die. Every relationship I encountered was attacked, whether black, white, young, or old, but I had to press on. If not for my family or me, for the ones who have suffered and were called home. Rest with Him, Eddie.

By the end of March, we were getting antsy and ready to go home to Charlotte. We made our countdown list, hoping it lined up with the doctors. We aimed to be back for Hannah's birthday in April, but the doctors have a set number of days before a bone marrow patient can go home. They finally gave the date – the day *after* Hannah's birthday - which was close enough. Hallelujah!

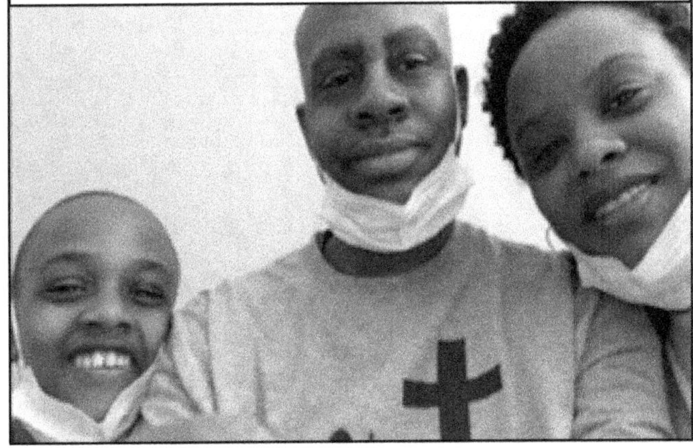

Felicia Davis is 😇 feeling blessed

...

with **Anthony Davis** at **Duke University Adult Bone Marrow Transplant Clinic**
April 18, 2017 (posted)

CHAPTER 12
My New Body

For we know that if the earthly tent which is our house is torn down, we have a building from God, a house not made with hands, eternal in the heavens.

2 Corinthians 5:1

A believer is someone who deems Jesus as our Lord and Savior and knows that He died on the cross for our sins. Once you realize that, our earthly tent (our body) becomes a residential temple for the Holy Spirit. When that occurs, we must build on our purpose and grow in our faith. It sounds like a lot, but we start as babes in Christ, and as we rely on God, we allow Him to work through us while we let go of earthly constructs. We mature where we stand, firm on our beliefs.

DUKE CLINIC

Since I had been going through this process, I found it very tough visiting the clinic, feeling GREAT, and watching my fellow "transplanters" struggle. I was sitting there waiting to be called for labs, and EMTs came in with a stretcher and went back to the treatment area to pick up a patient. I was hoping to avoid seeing them bring a lifeless body out because I did not want to get depressed. I was joking with Nurse Pearl as she took my weight and prepared me for my vitals and labs. I said, "Take your time Ms. Pearl," while thinking about what could happen; Lord *knows* I did not want to see that stretcher. I have these "thorns" that are constant reminders of where I came from, but I must face my fears and allow God to use me through them.

About 10-15 minutes later, my labs were done, and I had to return to the waiting area before the next phase – seeing Dr. Lopez. How do I say GOD IS GOOD while others suffer without sounding selfish? I will proclaim it the way I think He wants me to say it... GOD IS GOOD!

We often complain about God showing up late but understand this; we serve an on-time God! About 5 minutes after I sat in the waiting room, I looked up, and the EMTs were rolling a young man on a stretcher. He was awake! I do not know his situation, but I knew *something* was wrong because he was on that stretcher, but the main thing was he was alive.

A few minutes later, a lady was walking with her husband coming from treatment. She was struggling to walk, but her husband helped her. I mentioned these people because I am incredibly grateful for what God has done for me. I would be a liar if I told you my walk is much easier than theirs – it is NOT! But now that I am in complete remission, I believe God continues to allow me to see others suffering to remind me of how far removed

I am from where I started in this process. He knows me. The book's purpose is to allow people to see what God has done for me to encourage them. And with this inspiration comes freedom. So, when I am inspired, I move.

MATTHEWS CLINIC

Monday, July 3, 2017, I had to go to the clinic in Matthews to get lab work done. Like the clinic at Duke, sometimes the difficulty lies where I can see that the other patients there aren't doing as well as I am. Today was more demanding than most. I am in the waiting area waiting for the results of my blood work, and an older gentleman was being escorted in a wheelchair by his son. His son places him in the waiting area across from a lady expecting her husband to return from his treatment. The son sat down next to his father and started to talk to him. The father appeared confused and began asking the lady questions about what she is done in the clinic.

Just then, I received a text from Felicia to text her
after I was finished, but I thought it was better to call her.
So, I had one ear listening to Felicia and the other
listening to the man in the wheelchair. The man started
complaining about everything: the different chemo
treatments, the infusion, his deteriorating health. His son
mouthed to the lady, "I'm sorry." Then the man started
crying. I guess the lady could not deal with it, so she got
up and went to be with her husband. I cannot say I blame

Anthony Davis is with **Paulus Ford** · · ·
Jun 26, 2017 (posted)

If you are in the Charlotte area this Saturday (7/1) at 9am, join
the men of New Beginnings at our Men's Breakfast Fellowship.
Food, Fellowship, a Powerful Word and it's FREE!

her because she has her issues
and her husband's cancer to
worry about. I got off the
phone with Felicia and told her
I would talk to her later.

After the woman left, I started listening to the son's conversation with his father. The son was great. He was trying to stay positive, reminding him of people in the family who have been through stuff, and he helped them. Then the man said the word MIRACLE - one of my trigger words. The son then gets up to see someone he recognizes. The man backs up, turns around, sees me, and jumps – he was unaware I was sitting there. I started to talk to him.

Before all this "stuff," I would have just waited for my results and left. I would not interject into strangers' conversations; I would just go without saying a word. Now, when God presents opportunities, I respond. God had both of us there for a reason. I proceeded to talk to him about my testimony. When his son returned, he recognized me and said, "You're from New Beginnings; at the Men's Breakfast, you shared your testimony." (Rev. Paulus asked me to tell my testimony at our yearly Men's

Ministry Breakfast Fellowship.). I acknowledged the son's inquiry and continued to talk to his father about not worrying - which, as believers, we do too much of.

The Bible says that God takes care of the birds. That is, He provides food, shelter, and covering. Those are the things we worry about – providing for ourselves and our families. But if that is the *only* thing we worry about and God already has that covered, then there is NOTHING to worry about…NOTHING!

I told him he has a good son and needs more people around him like his son to speak positively into his life. I knew that he had more positive people in his life because his son learned it from somebody. I also shared with him that we must use the miracles that we read about in the Bible, see in our families, and hear through testimonies as building blocks for our faith.

The son's wife walks in, and he tells her, "This was the guy I was telling you about. He was the one who spoke on his testimony at the Men's Breakfast." As Christians, we need to always be on point. We never know who is in our presence and how we can affect them. The son's statement validated everything I was telling his father. The son needed to be at the Men's breakfast, and I had to be at the clinic for the father.

My results came in, and it was time for me to leave. I shook the father's hand and told him that this was his assignment, and God trusted him with it. A few nurses were around us by then, and I sensed a "Hallelujah!" moment coming on. As I sat in my car, my emotions got the best of me – I felt the presence of the Holy Spirit. I was in awe. The longer I went through this journey, the more the whole shebang started to add up. Every day of my life led to everything I was experiencing – which assisted me in this test turned testimony. Again, not an accident; this was PURPOSE.

A few months passed, and I was at a restaurant to pick up some food. I held my arm back to hold the door for a man trailing me. He said, "Hey, how are you doing?" I responded kindly. He said, "You don't remember me, do you?" It took me a minute, but I said, "You were at the clinic with your dad." He said, "He was my father-in-law." Not recognizing the verb tense, I asked him, "How's he doing?" He said, "He passed." I empathically said, "I'm sorry to hear that." He then thanked me for the words I spoke to his father-in-law and how inspiring they were to him.

One of Pastor Henderson's sermon topics was "Keep Talking - They're Not Going to Listen - Keep Talking." Pastor said he was instructed to speak on these verses because someone needed to hear the message again. The meat of the message was not intended for me, but the act of repeating the message - preached many times before by him - was.

Lately, I have felt like my testimony is becoming redundant, and people are tired (or will soon tire) of seeing and hearing about it. But I believe that God wants me to continue spreading this miracle story. Which led me to Noah:

Noah did according to all that the Lord had commanded him.

Genesis 7:5

God told Noah a flood was coming, and he had to build an ark to save himself, his family, and some animals (just paraphrasing). For over 100 years, Noah built the ark and told people the same "Flood" story. Tell your story and keep talking - even if you think they are not listening. Not because you want to, but because God commanded you to do so.

For me, leukemia has been a blessing. Something meant to take me out allowed me to be a blessing to people and for people to be a blessing to me. As I reminisce, the journey solidified my belief in God – He *is* a Healer. It was my confirmation that Jesus is my Savior – He died for me. The Holy Spirit resides in me – He speaks to *and* guides me.

> *"Before I formed you in the womb I knew you, and before you were born I consecrated you; I have appointed you a prophet to the nations."*
>
> *Jeremiah 1:5*

If you personalize this scripture, let it stoke in you a reason for being alive. When I graduated from Ministers in Training, this was the Bible verse I chose for my testimony. It remains one of my favorite scriptures because of its direct correlation to *purpose*. Before an inventor forms their creation, they already know why. Think about it; God is The Creator. Before you were made, God knew you, and before you were born, God set you apart; He appointed you for something specific. You have a purpose. God has an assignment for you. He is not silent; He is constantly talking to you. Remove those things that are blocking you from hearing Him. Use my testimony as proof that He exists. Believe me when I say,

"Be obedient to His word and watch." And after He works in your life, then tell someone your story.

To this day, I observe, listen, and apply. I encourage you to embrace everything and everyone who crosses your path and to use those encounters to achieve *your* purpose.

Be Blessed!!

MY LOVE LIST

The following is a list of family and friends who stopped by for a visit while I was at Wake Forest Baptist Hospital, Duke University Hospital, and the apartment in Durham, NC. They all went out of their way to show me some love and are forever part of my Love List.

WAKE FOREST BAPTIST HOSPITAL
AUGUST / SEPTEMBER / OCTOBER 2016

Jamier Aiken Jr.	Rev. Paulus Ford	Sharon Rivera
Pat Barrett	Kevin Green	Vinnie Rivera
Stewart Barrett Jr.	Min. Merica Greene	Min. Kevin Rivers
Stewart Barrett Sr.	Dennis Griffith	Min. Willette Robinson
Marilyn Dabney	Vanessa Griffith	Sharon Robinson
Constance "Ma" Davis	Min. Reggie Hobson	Will Robinson
Glenn Davis	Daniella Jones	Donnie Saunders
Kathy Davis	Min. Donteia King	Angela Tatum
Valorie Davis	Min. Keith King	Troy Tatum
Herb Downing	Roxie Latimer	Min. Tami Ward
Min. Tim Ellerbe	Ken Lewis	Shaquirah Ward
James "Pop" Ellison	Min. Rose Ling	Min. Kevin Watkins
Thomasine "Mom" Ellison	Dennis Porch	Perfect White
Camile Felisbret	Okemia Porch	Min. Brandi Williams
Cherrie Felisbret	Marsha Purnell	Min. Freddie Williams
Jason Felisbret		

DUKE UNIVERSITY & DURHAM
JANUARY / FEBRUARY / MARCH / APRIL 2017

Constance "Ma" Davis	Vanessa Knight	Vinnie Rivera
Glenn Davis	Min. Rose Ling	Min. Gloria Story
Kathy Davis	Aunt Emma McPherson	Stan Walker
Valorie Davis	Min. Carolyn Neal	Ericka Walker
Daniella Jones	Melissa Paulin	Iris Walker
Marcia Jones	Dennis Porch	Solomon Walker
Min. Trent Knight	Okemia Porch	

www.ingramcontent.com/pod-product-compliance
Lightning Source LLC
Chambersburg PA
CBHW072227150726
48002CB00005B/1969